MILES DAVIS

MILES DAVIS

A MUSICAL BIOGRAPHY

by Bill Cole

MORROW QUILL PAPERBACKS
NEW YORK 1974

Library of Congress Cataloging in Publication Data

Cole, Bill, (date)
  Miles Davis: a musical biography.

  "Morrow quill paperbacks."

  Revision of the author's thesis (M.A.), University
of Pittsburgh 1970.
  Reprint of the ed. published by W. Morrow, New York.
  Bibliography: p.
  Includes index.
  1. Davis, Miles.   2. Jazz musicians—United States
—Biography.
[ML419.D39C6   1980]   788'.1'0924 [B]   80-14306
ISBN 0-688-05203-7

Printed in the United States of America

     2   3   4   5   6   7   8   9   10

To Linda, Atticus, and Zena

Preface

This book is an outgrowth of the paper done as partial fulfillment for my M. A. degree from the University of Pittsburgh, completed in 1970. It represents first a fantasy, then a solid idea, then a reality which has lasted over twenty-two years. The text itself is in three parts: an introduction which explains the time period encompassing Miles Davis' musical history up until this date, a musical biography which deals with Miles's bands and those who influenced him and his music, and a scrutiny of his style which describes the evolution of his musicianship. There are also a bibliography, a list of recording sessions, and transcriptions of some of Miles's recorded solos which can act only as a guide and not take the place of listening to his music. This book purposely does not provide tidbits about Miles's personal life, but deals strictly with his life as an African-American musician practicing African-American music.

There are three brothers who have had a decided

hand in shaping the musical thoughts I present in this book. Nathan Davis (Assistant Professor of Music), my academic adviser for my Master's paper at the University of Pittsburgh, was my first African-American teacher in the established American educational institution after twenty years (including kindergarten) of experiencing that system. I had become so defeated by that system that when I first came in contact with him, I had just about given up music. (One can't really give up music, but I had resigned myself to being a well-informed listener.) Nathan Davis' encouragement enabled me to start and finish the paper and, if it hadn't been for his confidence in me, I probably would have become another slave trying to make it in somebody's meat factory. The second man is Clifford Thornton (Assistant Professor of Music), my Ph.D. adviser at Wesleyan University, who literally put an instrument in my hands and told me to learn to play it. Our numerous conversations together and his many references in music helped me to shape this book in my own mind. Most of all, his patience with my impatience provided the musical discipline necessary for this work. And Sam Rivers, the visiting artist in African-American music at Wesleyan University, showed me the possibilities of collective improvisation which further extended the potential I saw in the music of my people.

This book is a manifestation of a long struggle to find some medium in which to express my own thoughts about music. It should be prefaced by the fact that, as a victim of racism in all its peculiar ramifications, I have found the music of African-American people to be a great source of strength. Miles Davis's music has undeniably been one specific source of that strength. Although it is difficult to communicate literally a nonliterary mechanism, I have attempted to describe that source in musical terms. I would say that this book would be useless without all of Miles's music or, at least, that which is documented.

Finally, I want to thank Nancy Holzapfel, who helped with the research and editing, and my wife, Linda, whose strength and perseverance helped create this effort.

Contents

INTRODUCTION

A friend told me
He'd risen above jazz.
I leave him there.

for Miles Davis

—Michael Harper [1]

It has been several years now since I first read the above poem by brother Michael Harper when it appeared in a collection published about the same time Miles's *Bitches Brew* was released. At that time, there was no question in my mind that this poem was written for Miles; now I teeter between for Miles or about him.

In the fifties, when I was a teenager, Miles was the "main man." The "hip" blacks had all of his albums, and many, like myself, emulated his every gesture; one

---

[1] Michael Harper, *Dear John, Dear Coltrane* (U. of Pittsburgh Press, Pittsburgh, Pa., 1970), p. 5.

of my friends went as far as wearing a corduroy suit and small apple cap similar to the one Miles wears on the cover of *Musing*. By the time I was eighteen (1956), I had memorized all of his solos and could recognize his playing among a host of trumpeters. Later, when I owned a record shop for a short time, it was called Musing, so great was my love for his music.

When Miles Davis sought experience in bebop, he selected the very best teachers of that era to teach him. This was his apprentice period, and he chose as his master teacher Charlie Parker ("Bird"), the most prodigious innovator of that style. One of the consistent things about Davis is the high level of musicianship present in all of his collaborators. Some people may mistakenly think that Miles Davis just arrived, that he didn't evolve. Nothing could be further from the truth.

Bop (*ca.* 1939–1951) was an enigmatic period in the history of African-American music. It developed into a black music aesthetic, one that was a total conscious effort to liberate the music of African-American people. It led directly to the music of Ornette Coleman and John Coltrane, and its influence is just beginning to crease skulls. Reaction dominated the so-called jazz criticism of this period, and shouts of "Heresy!" "Weird!" and "Misguided!" filled the reviews. But the pioneers of bop seemed oblivious to their critics and audience. After all, they were artists, not entertainers, and as long as the criticism amounted to an uninformed subjective analysis of the music, they felt no responsibility to it.

Almost immediately, Charlie Parker recognized that there was no copyright protecting harmonic progressions in any given piece, so he led the field writing melodies to given progressions. "Cherokee" was transformed into "Ko-Ko," "How High the Moon" became "Ornithology," and "Home in Indiana" became "Donna Lee." Even Miles got into the act by writing "Dig," which has the same chord progression as "Sweet Georgia Brown." For the most part, these new melodies were medium- and up-tempo with jagged lines and wide intervallic relationships. Unquestionably the style was antilyrical; confrontation was definitely in vogue.

Harmonically, 7th chords were commonplace, and 9th, 11th, and 13th chords cropped up everywhere. Many times the upper intervals took the place of the traditional chord, using all of its inversions. A C^7 might become a B^{b7} in the second inversion in the second chorus. Pianists like Thelonious Monk, Tadd Dameron, and later Bud Powell would never hesitate to use substitutions, to alternate chords, or to build expanded chords. "Dizzy" Gillespie knew the piano and demonstrated his harmonic knowledge in his trumpet improvisations. He was the person who encouraged Miles to learn to play the piano.

During bop, musicianship really began to blossom. Revolutionary changes redefined the responsibility of certain instruments in combination with others. The bass carried the pulse, freeing the piano to expand and experiment harmonically. It became a truly pizzicato instrument with its players, such as Jimmy Blanton, developing more finger dexterity than was previously thought possible. Drummers related to the new polyrhythms with paralleling techniques: accommodating the increases in tempos, they began to use the cymbals to keep time instead of the "sock" (bass drum). This allowed both legs to be free, changing accents, while the tempo became more and more implied. Skill and inventiveness in duration is always the hallmark of an African-descended music.

Bird and Diz were, and Diz still is, master musicians. On November 26, 1945, the famous recording of "Ko-Ko" was made. On this date, Miles couldn't play the "head" (actual melody) of the piece, so Gillespie accepted the mandate of playing not only the piano, but also the "head" on muted trumpet. Playing only this melody and the improvised bridge, which were two very short episodes, he demonstrated his control over both registers with twists and turns, jumping from high to low and back at will. He had great anticipation, lagging behind the beat and bursting out with phrases of outstanding rhythmic interest. His articulation was, and always is, flawless, never stumbling to a note or through a phrase. It was Gillespie and his advanced ideas about rhythm that brought the Afro-Cuban percussionist Chano Pozo to the United States. This fact has been glossed over by most historians of African-American music, but if today's interest in the roots and, especially, traditional rhythms of Africa is any indication of their importance, then this move by Gillespie in 1947 becomes more and more significant. Pozo, not only a gifted percussionist, but also a student of West African multirhythmic drumming, belonged to Abakwa, a Nigerian cult group based in Cuba which provided performers for the Mardi Gras in Havana each year.

Diz defied traditional blowing techniques, extending his cheeks and neck, looking as if he were about to burst when he played. In the early fifties he changed the narrow bore which extends out to the bell of the trumpet, bending it to a 60° angle for reasons only he

will ever know. His manner of dress during the forties
—the horn-rimmed glasses, beret, and goatee—probably
labeled him more of an entertainer than a serious con-
tributor to that era; but it was only the immensity of
Parker's talent that kept Gillespie from being the leading chronicler of that time. Dizzy has not only influenced every trumpeter from that time on, he has also
expanded possibilities for pianists through his knowledge of harmony and for percussionists through his use
of rhythm, for the reasons already mentioned.

Thirty-three years after his initial impact and
eighteen after his death, there is still no way of mea-
suring Parker's total contribution to African-American
music. There are so many stories about him, but the
one I like best recalls when he first turned professional
and was playing in a band with Jo Jones as the drummer. His playing was so lousy that Jones took one of
the cymbals off his trap set and threw it at him. The
story goes on to reveal that, after this happened, Parker
"woodshedded" in the Ozark Mountains of Missouri for
a year and when he returned on the musical scene he
was formidable. In fact he was so formidable that, almost singlehandedly, he completely turned everybody
around about the possibilities of African-American
music. He mastered every facet of the game by looking
inside a structure, reshaping it, and producing a revolutionary, artistic work. He took a music which was
being choked to death by the thickly arranged, rhythmically dull, European-inspired dance music of the
swing bands and transformed it into an energetic music
second to none in the world. He brought the music back
to the people.

I was never privileged to hear Parker in person, so
the only testimony I have is his recordings. He always

had impeccable musicianship, and he often left the other musicians dragging; he was also very well practiced. The melodic lines he composed jumped and skipped so often that it must have been hard to remember the lines and, therefore, difficult to count the choruses. Drummer Dave Tough recalls that he was scared when he first realized this about bop players.[2] The up-tempos at which Parker played changed the entire concept of trap drumming. He had what all genius musicians have, a unique sense of duration. He knew how to put music together.

Parker was born in Kansas City when that town was bursting with outstanding blues bands. He apprenticed in one of the best, Jay McShann's band. Bird was a strong blues player, and, in spite of all the revolutionary processes he brought to the music, his playing was always saturated with that essential element. The blues has always defied Western musicological definition. Imamu Amiri Baraka called his book *Blues People* with an appropriate subtitle, "The Negro Experience in White America and the Music That Developed from It." The blues is essentially a way of looking at life by a people who descended from Africa. It is oral rather than literate in its transmission. Spontaneity, the impromptu shout or holler, whether expressing sadness or joy, is its essential characteristic.

Blues forms have evolved, but they are not absolute. There are the 8-, 12-, 16-, and accompanying 24- and 32-bar motifs, and most of the time they follow some variant of the A-A-B-A melodic input. There certainly is what Ortiz Walton calls the "juxtaposition of major upon minor tonality" which creates the "funki-

[2] Henry Pleasants, *Serious Music—And All That Jazz* (Simon and Schuster, N. Y., 1969), p. 138.

ness"[3] of the music. This juxtaposition usually comes in the improvisation. The intertwining of lowered 3rds, 5ths, 6ths, and 7ths in any given scale provides the music with that earthy feeling that is so characteristic of the blues. Sometimes the sounding of a note together with its raised or lowered half-step also produces the same effect. One can also say the blues evolved from the tonic—sub-dominant—dominant—tonic structures to the more complex variations of this principle utilized in bebop. That is, the blues evolved through a harmonically modulating system, or harmonic movement.

All the literate treatises on the planet could not actually explain the blues. Parker's "Scrapple from the Apple" is a 32-bar blues with an A-A-B-A form. The B section is actually a series of progressions on which to improvise, something that Parker was fond of doing in his pieces. The progressions in A are II^7 to V^7 for four bars, then hitting the tonic at the fifth, back to a quick II^7 to V^7, then to I. The B part is a I-IV-V^7 progression leading into the II^7 of A. This is a standard pop tune form, and, in the hands of a person unfamiliar with the nuances of the blues, the oral nuances, it would sound like just another pop tune. In the hands of Bird it is manifested as a certain timbre, metronome sense, rhythmic quality, directness, and that old intangible "feeling" which emanates from hundreds of African-American communities throughout the country.

The blues is not taught in the European-inspired American academy. It is usually held in contempt there. Perhaps this is because it is uncontrollable music; without warning, it can burst and scream, arousing the spirits of the people. Its practitioners use seemingly in-

---

[3] Ortiz Walton, *Music: Black, White, and Blue* (William Morrow and Co., Inc., N.Y., 1972), p. 32.

correct blowing techniques, but it has been these means
that have freed the music. When Miles Davis first went
to New York, he enrolled at the Juilliard School of
Music; however, his real mission in that city was to
study with Charlie Parker, who was working there at
the time. One of the oldest still-functioning processes
of African-American music is the master-teacher/stu-
dent relationship, which goes as far back as Africa.
The student learns all he can by "hanging out," carrying established musicians' horn cases while picking up
all the information he can. Anyone wanting to play
this music must first learn to play the blues and then
pay the dues.

Bop wasn't a music embraced by the general public. Most of its innovators suffered severely, economically, and in many other ways. Charlie Christian, who
pioneered linear guitar playing, died when he was
twenty-three of tuberculosis. The aforementioned
Jimmy Blanton died when he was twenty-one, also
of tuberculosis. Parker was only thirty-four when he
died. Pianist Thelonious Monk spent ten years unable
to work in New York City because his cabaret card was
taken away from him by the police, allegedly for a
drug violation. Much to the chagrin of many dancers,
bop created a sit-down audience. It emerged in the
after-hours at Minton's playhouse in Harlem and was
relegated to the nightclub culture of alcoholics, pros-
titutes, and heavy drug users. Bop struggled hard and
survived, radically changing the music and the life
styles of its practitioners.

After bop, Miles slipped briefly, and his dabbling
initiated the so-called "cool" period, which provided a
forum for many of its European imitators. However,
Miles soon blossomed and became the leading voice

of the fifties. Bebop matured also in the fifties and was renamed hard bop. And, as has always been the case throughout the history of African-American music, white musicians created their own watered-down versions of the music called, at various times, "cool," "West Coast," and "progressive" jazz. Soon a fierce monetary competitiveness began to grow. There was also a sudden return to the roots of African-American music: church music and the blues. The small bands, consisting of four or five instrumentalists, which pioneered in the forties, began to flourish. The Modern Jazz Quartet, the Jazz Messengers, the Max Roach/Clifford Brown Quintet, and other similar-sized groups formed everywhere. Using the basic patterns developed in the forties, only now with a rounder, harder tone, improvisations became longer and individual stylization predominated. Charlie Parker died in 1955, just two years after he and Diz, along with a rhythm section which included three younger musicians—Bud Powell (piano), Charlie Mingus (bass), and Max Roach (percussion)—gave a landmark concert at Massey Hall in Toronto. After Parker died, everything was up for grabs.

If bebop reaffirmed the possibilities of the music, adapting revolutionary processes to traditional African-American forms, hard bop reinforced the legitimacy of these processes by exhausting European harmonic capabilities. Overall musicianship had to catch up to the few technically proficient instrumentalists able to deal with the frantic tempos of bebop. Hard bop allowed for this transition; tempos decreased in speed, and the music became more lyrical. This deceleration was compensated by the longer improvisation. Musicians were now free to take as many choruses as they wanted. I don't mean to imply that the lines of bebop were being filtered or even diluted during hard bop. Sonny Rollins' "Doxy," Jackie McLean's "Little Melonae," Horace Silver's "Quicksilver," and Miles's "Tune Up" are all great pieces with lines patterned after bebop. But hard bop also ushered in the organ trio and the "funky" sound, both indicating a conservative trend which lasted only a very short time. It may sound crazy, but even in the dress of the practitioners, a conservative tendency seemed to be prominent. Dress during the bebop era was, at the very least, flamboyant, but hard bop brought about bands whose members wore identical dark blue suits, very Ivy-League. In studying the evolution of any music, one always discovers a revolutionary period when all traditional mechanisms are assaulted, followed by a period dominated by examination of those changes. The great pressure African-American musicians have always felt constantly to change the music, pressure brought to bear by a country which has never developed culture and exploits all the arts, only attests to the durability and creativity inherent in the music.

There was and still is a large audience for hard bop. New York City, which provided the core ever since Minton's, had "jazz" clubs in every borough. The critics got uptight when the strongest bands were all black, so they began to call it "Crow Jimism." Such reactions only make clearer the contradiction in the fact that symphony orchestras discriminate blatantly while artistic African-American music is expected to be integrated. As a matter of fact, exploitation of African-American musicians was at an all-time high. Some of the record companies who had recording contracts with the younger, fresher playing talent took advantage of these musicians' lack of business sense by producing many records without providing the proper royalties.

And because so many of the performers were heavy drug users and alcoholics, they were easy prey to such victimizations. Fortunately, Charlie Parker, for all of his excesses, was a very astute businessman, but this fact was not transmitted to the fifties until Miles made his big splash in 1955.

Brass players, who for such a long time had dominated the music but were overshadowed in the thirties by Coleman Hawkins and Lester Young and then in the forties by Parker, emerged again. Not only trumpeters but trombonists such as J. J. Johnson, Jimmy Cleveland, and, later, Curtis Fuller and Julian Priester made substantial contributions to the music. J. J., with his fluid style, opened up new horizons for others to explore; but, sadly enough, there haven't been too many followers, since the trombone is a difficult instrument to master as well as a somewhat cumbersome instrument to play. Even the French horn got into the act when Julius Watkins and tenor saxophonist Charlie Rouse fronted a quintet in the mid-fifties. But the trumpet prevailed. Influenced by Diz and "Fats" Navarro, a long line of trumpeters paraded through this decade, each with outstanding facilities. The list includes Miles, Clifford Brown, Kenny Dorham, and later Lee Morgan, Freddie Hubbard, Donald Byrd, and Booker Little.

Clifford Brown was, even in this outstanding group, the most gifted. He had complete control of his horn at all times; he was clean, didn't smoke or drink, and had beautiful vibrations. Like Diz, he had a blowing technique which was slightly exaggerated, but he could play line after line of fresh ideas. His staccato bounced, and, like all the great geniuses of this music, he had a unique sense of duration. Brown also played with great lyricism and a very pure but stylized sound. He was, of course, a very casual blues player. The communication that went on between him and Max Roach when they had their band in the mid-fifties was a wonderful thing to witness. They had great admiration for one another, so Max was obviously greatly affected by Clifford's death.[4] Fortunately, Clifford made many records which attest to his brilliance.

Booker Little came along late in the fifties and, like Brown, had a short tenure. He was probably the first "new" music trumpeter and had a longtime association with alto saxophonist Eric Dolphy. It is folly to speculate how the music would have been directed if Brown and Little had lived to realize their potentials, but their talents were considerable. Tenor player Harold Land was the other horn in that Max Roach/Clifford Brown band, but he didn't provide the musical stimulation that Eric Dolphy projected night after night for Little. So, even in the very sparse recording material Little left, one can get insight into his creative energy. His playing was a lot like Brown's, but his lines were more complex in the context of the tonality. He never thought in terms of wrong notes, only of how music can best be expressed. Little died at the age of twenty-three.

The few new music situations that began to develop in the mid-fifties were mostly underground. Sun Ra was beginning his revolutionary bands in Chicago at about this time, and Charlie Mingus had started his Jazz Workshops in New York. But this was a period to acclaim the masters of the forties. Many of the

---

[4] Bassist Art Davis has some interesting comments on the hazards of being a so-called jazz musician in an interview with Joe Ubiles, *Black Creation*, Fall 1972, pp. 22–24.

students of bop (Jackie McLean, Sonny Rollins, Milt Jackson, Jimmy Heath, Horace Silver, etc.) were beginning to be heard frequently either through public appearances or recordings. Finally, Thelonious Monk received the long-overdue acclaim for his inventive harmonic constructions and his accompanying rhythmatic ideas. Most significantly, the fifties produced John Coltrane, who eventually give credence to the "new" music of the sixties.

If Miles had done nothing else but study with Parker and provide a forum for John Coltrane, his name would still go down as an important advocate of this music. "Trane" moved the music in so many positive directions that it is hard to describe his impact. He was totally committed to creating the most viable music possible, but only after he exhausted the potential of hard bop. He never compromised his style to accommodate the vicious, irresponsible attacks of critics. When I first saw him in Miles's band, I was dumbfounded by his abandonment of anything that represented a pure sound. He was always an aggressive player, and if Bird brought the eighth note to bebop, Trane certainly brought the sixteenth and thirty-second to hard bop. It seems incredible that a music which is treated with such disdain in its own country should produce two such extraordinarily endowed musicians.

Things happened quickly from the middle to the end of the fifties. Mingus recorded an outstanding piece called "Pithecanthropus Erectus," which had some "free" playing by Jackie McLean and J. R. Montrose. Miles began working more and more with modal structures, pieces with fewer chord changes. There was a star-crossed attempt to consciously combine European classical music and so-called jazz, actively supported by

John Lewis and Gunther Schuller, but it failed miserably. It was called Third Stream music.

People who try to superimpose on a music structures which oppose its basic concepts usually fail. In all of its complex idioms, African-American music is the music of the people. It is African-American because it is descended from Africa, sustained by rhythm, call and response forms, and the blues scale, and applies non-Western timbre techniques to Western instruments. It is a nonliterate music, although it is true that to develop an aesthetic, master musicians like Bird and Trane saw the need to investigate thoroughly the instruments that they were using; this involved a thorough scrutiny of the musical system that produced them. All the new applications they made related to rhythm and other African communication forms were expressed from the time the first slave picked up a Western instrument. The evolution appears slow, but only when taken out of its historical context. It was given a good, hard, swift kick by Charlie Parker; had he lived, it would have been liberated faster. The lifespan of many of our black geniuses has been short, but there have been many. This has been one of the real tests of the durability and the resilience of our music.

Ornette Coleman took the music off, although there are some who say that Charlie Haden (bass) and Edward Blackwell (percussion) provided the canvas for Ornette and Don Cherry to paint. His arrival certainly was revolutionary, but it was Trane who dominated the whole scene from 1957 until he died in 1967. He continued to grow, with each record indicating progress, searching, unlimited expansion. Just before Coltrane died, in the spring of 1967, there was a concert at Carnegie Hall in New York City called "Titans of the Tenor." Trane, Sonny Rollins, Coleman Hawkins, Thelonious Monk with Charlie Rouse, and Yusef Lateef were invited to perform with their own bands. Trane brought a band that included Pharaoh Sanders (tenor), Don Ayler (trumpet), McCoy Tyner (piano), Jimmy Garrison (bass), Rashied Ali (percussion), and Albert Ayler (tenor). The producers agreed to all except Albert Ayler, but Coltrane was so insistent on having all the great tenor players there that he paid Albert out of his own pocket. That was the quality of the man, always surrounding himself with younger, searching musicians.

Miles Davis has survived almost thirty years in one of the worst musical atmospheres in the world. Most of those years were uncompromising ones, but in the early sixties he began, for no reason or purpose, to make some negative criticism against obviously outstanding musicians such as Eric Dolphy. His bands still had fine personnel, but they stagnated, and the relationship between him and the other members became essentially a business arrangement. Most of the rehearsals were among the sidemen rather than with the whole band together. However, Miles's playing continues to be on the highest level, still that penetrating sound that burns through one as phenol burns through the skin. The music has passed him by and now he seems to be more concerned about playing for rock audiences than for the people. But there's no telling about Miles Davis. He, more than anyone else, has had the admiration of the black brothers on the street, and he has this capacity to regroup and regenerate. His contribution to our music and his stature as a man will always mean a great deal to African-American people.

BIOGRAPHY

Miles Dewey Davis III was born on May 5, 1926 (Taurus), in Alton, Illinois. Alton is a small industrial city just northeast of St. Louis on the Mississippi River. History remembers it as the final city of the Lincoln-Douglas debates. When Miles was less than a year old his family moved to East St. Louis, Illinois. "About the first thing I can remember as a little boy was a white man running me down the street hollering, 'Nigger! Nigger!' "[5] Whatever attitudes he might have formed as an adult about his reality were seeded in experiences similar to this one. His father, a dentist, years later recalled this incident: "When Miles III was in grade school we moved into an all-white neighborhood. A white man once told him it was no nigger street and drove him from it. I got my shotgun but I could never

[5] Don DeMichael, "Miles Davis," Rolling Stone, December 13, 1969, p. 23.

find him. I don't think Miles, a sensitive boy, ever forgot it, or our troubles." [6]

In 1917, East St. Louis was the scene of at least forty African-Americans losing their lives in a riot that grew out of the employment of African-Americans in a factory holding government contracts. African-Americans were stabbed, clubbed and hanged; and one two-year-old child was shot and thrown in the doorway of a burning building.[7] Obviously a city with this kind of recent history would not be too receptive to an African-American family moving into one of its white neighborhoods; having grown up in a neighborhood like that myself, I can imagine the humiliation Miles must have suffered.

Miles's father was not only a respected dentist but also a prosperous landowner. Therefore, unlike most of his contemporaries, Miles didn't feel the economic pains early. The so-called middle-class African-American demonstrates one of this country's glaring contradictions in his quest for money in a structure where all the institutions are racist. Dr. Davis remembered his own lineage and told how Miles handled those early abrasions:

> By genetics and breeding Miles is always going to be ahead of his time. Historically way back into slavery days, the Davises have been musicians and performed classical works in the homes of the plantation owners. My father, Miles I, was born six years after the Emancipation and forbade me to play music because the only place a Negro could play then was in barrel houses. My father

[6] Marc Crawford, "Miles Davis: Evil Genius of Jazz," *Ebony*, January 1961, p. 70.

[7] John Hope Franklin, *From Slavery to Freedom: A History of American Negroes* (New York: Alfred A. Knopf, Inc., 1967), p. 474.

was the most efficient double entry column book-
keeper in Arkansas before the coming of the adding machine and white men came to his home
under cover of night for him to fix their books.
He was later driven from his extensive holdings.
    . . . [Miles] liked long walks in the country,
hunting and fishing. He was an excellent horseman
and if he was ever thrown he'd remount immediately and master his mount. When he was in high
school he played trumpet. In school competitions
he was always the best, but the blue-eyed boys
always won first and second prizes. Miles had always to settle for third. The officials, Miles and
everybody else knew he should have had first
prize. You can't treat a kid like that and tell him
to come out and say the water wasn't dirty.[8]

So the long, strong musical heritage was temporarily broken by Miles I and Miles II but obviously not
forgotten. Miles III picked up that heritage, and in
spite of a few early setbacks, not because of his ability
but because of the color of his skin, he stayed with it.

Miles began playing trumpet in grade school.
Every day at school, just before it was time to go home,
he and some other students practiced holding one note
for long periods of time. This bored him, but just at
the right time, the time when young kids can tire of
uninspired, tedious drilling and lose their enthusiasm
for music, a friend of his father brought him a trumpet
and showed him how to play the chromatic scale. Miles
always had a good ear, and learning how to play the
chromatic scale increased his awareness of the space
between half-steps, which awareness he exploited to its
fullest when he became a professional.

[8] Crawford, "Miles Davis," p. 70.

Miles received his own horn when he was thirteen as a birthday gift from his father. (This was one of the many conflicts Miles saw between his mother and father. That is, his mother had wanted him to have a violin; Miles often thought that his father bought the trumpet more out of spite for his mother than anything else.) I can imagine what young Miles's first trumpet must have meant to him, since there is something special about a trumpet, saxophone, or set of drums to an African-American kid; these are the instruments with which we identify in the street, the instruments we see our favorite musicians "cattin' behind." It may seem chauvinistic to say so but African music is very overtly sexual, and so is the African-descended music in the Caribbean and South America. It follows that African-American music would be as sexually direct, but that it would be disguised because of the puritan posture of the country. So when Miles saw his new trumpet, he also saw all his boyhood fantasies begin to come to life.

Miles's first *real* teacher was Elwood Buchanan, a patient of his father's. Buchanan was a longtime St. Louis musician who taught Miles to play with no vibrato. " 'Play without any vibrato . . . You're gonna get old anyway and start shaking,' he used to say." [9] This practice accounts for the penetrating effect of the streams of lines Miles plays. Buchanan had seen all the great trumpeters who had come through St. Louis and most likely knew the young Clark Terry, who also grew up in that area. It was Buchanan who convinced Miles's father to buy him a trumpet instead of a violin, and later it was Buchanan who helped Miles to get his first professional gigs around St. Louis.

[9] Miles Davis, "Self-Portrait of the Artist" (New York: Columbia Records Press and Public Information, 1968), p. 2.

East St. Louis and the entire St. Louis area were Miles's initial professional playing areas. He started when he was sixteen in the Eddie Randall's Blue Devils Band. By that time Clark Terry was already well known, but had just gone off to the Navy. Miles had seen Clark a lot in a local drum and bugle corps, and playing their records back to back shows that Terry was Miles's first influence. It is really the strong early influences that help shape a musician's style; the first kind of sound a musician hears himself play and likes is usually the one he stays with. Later, when Miles realized that he wasn't going to be able to play like Diz or Fats Navarro, he fell back on the teachings of Buchanan and his first sound inspiration, Terry.

The Randall band offered Miles his first experience playing the blues. There were I-IV-V-I and II^7-V^7-I chord progressions which were easy for him to negotiate, as well as many variations on those basic models. There were plenty of good, bursting sounds coming from the band, and the vibrations with the audience were always positive. The Blue Devils were so well known in the St. Louis area that when out-of-town musicians played there, they would go out of their way to see this band. Miles began getting recognition, and when the Tiny Bradshaw band came through town, Sonny Stitt, who was with the band then, heard Miles and recommended him to Tiny. Miles, scared but determined, met with Bradshaw and the band: " 'The fellows in his band had their hair slicked down, they wore tuxedoes, and they offered me sixty whole dollars a week to play with them.' " [10] Sixty bucks in the early forties seemed as if it would be a gold mine in Miles's pocket, but his

[10] *Ibid.*

mother wouldn't have it. He was only sixteen and was going to finish high school. " 'I didn't talk to her for two weeks. And I didn't go with the band, either.' " [11]

Two years later Miles had his second musical experience with Charlie Parker. (His first one was when he was in high school.) Parker had spent his early childhood in Kansas City, directly across the state from St. Louis. Unlike Miles, Parker had a hard early life. He left school when he was fifteen and struggled in the street, which eventually left him an addict. His first professional experiences were disappointing, but his burning musical genius drove him to perfection, and soon he was held in awe by his contemporaries. The time was just right for Parker. All of the possibilities in the straight diatonic system had been exhausted and chromaticism was knocking at the door. Parker, looking to expand the possibilities, or the boundaries, to accommodate his ability, extended the chord to include all of its root possibilities. He knew that a D^7 resolved to G, but this scheme was no longer sufficient to deal with the complicated lines he heard in his head. Continuing along this path would mean only trying to improve on the styles of Johnny Hodges, Benny Carter, Roy Eldridge or Coleman Hawkins, which seemed fruitless to him. In other words, Parker found himself in the middle of an establishment, so he had either to imitate or to develop new rules. He chose the latter.

Parker was only six years Miles's senior, but more like sixty in terms of experience when he came through St. Louis in 1944 with Billy Eckstine's band. He made a lasting impression on the kid, who showed up opening night with a trumpet case under his arm. This band

[11] *Ibid.*

was the first of a series of bands Eckstine formed in the period from 1944 to 1947. From time to time over that period the personnel included Diz, Fats Navarro, Kenny Dorham, and Miles on trumpets; "Lucky" Thompson, Gene Ammons, Dexter Gordon, tenor saxes; Bird on alto and Leo Parker on baritone sax. The rhythm was John Malachi, piano, Art Blakey, percussion, and Tommy Potter on bass. Even more important than this exposure to other musicians, Miles had his first chance to see and play the inventive arrangements of the brilliant composer/arranger Tadd Dameron:

> . . . When we heard that they were coming to town, my friend and I were the first people in the hall, me with a trumpet under my arm. Diz walked up to me and said, "Kid, do you have a union card?" I said, "Sure." So I sat in with the band that night. I couldn't read a thing from listening to Diz and Bird. Then the third-trumpet man got sick. I knew the book because I loved the music so much I knew the third part by heart. So I played with the band for a couple of weeks. I had to go to New York then.[12]

It was a fantastic time for a young black man to try to realize his dream of becoming a top-flight musician. Miles remembered his mother's concern when he had wanted to go with Tiny Bradshaw, but he was in a better position now. He was eighteen, just about ready to finish high school, and equipped with an acceptance to the Juilliard School of Music in his pocket. His mother wanted him to go to Fisk University in Nashville. It took Miles almost a year to convince his father to allow him to go to New York, but he finally

---

[12] *Ibid.*, p. 3.

relented, much to the dismay of Mrs. Davis. So when Miles was nineteen, still naive but strong-willed, he arrived in New York City.

Since the early forties, New York City has been a challenging experience against which aspiring musicians must test their mettle. Los Angeles reaches high peaks once in a while, and Chicago keeps a steady level of excellent music, oriented toward the blues, but New York is where the conscious aesthetic evolved. It's not just that it gives musicians more chances to play, but rather that New York, being a gathering place for all the outstanding musicians, is naturally a conducive environment to learning; and if you want to learn how to play this music, you sure can't just read about it.

Miles had mixed feelings about Juilliard. He had really gone to New York to try to hook up with Parker and spent his whole first month's allowance just trying to find Bird. Juilliard is a very demanding school, but it is also one of the best practical schools in the country. Studying there for four years could teach one a great deal about music, but there would be nothing African-American going on in it. Miles found himself among a lot of trumpeters who had learned to play exactly opposite the way he had learned. They were encouraged to develop not an individual sound, but one with much vibrato, after a standard model. Most of his fellow student couldn't improvise (and really were not interested in doing so) but were excellent sight readers. In this context Miles found himself deficient.

One semester at Juilliard was enough for Miles, one of the few of his contemporaries to study music in one of America's credential-giving institutions. But " '. . . all that shit they were teaching wasn't doing

me a damn bit of good. . . .' " [13] He caught up with
Parker and Diz shortly after his first month in New
York and, on the advice of Gillespie, he used the practice rooms at Juilliard to learn to play the piano. He
also worked out the chords under the lines he heard
Parker play the night before, having written down the
improvisations on matchbook covers.[14]

Miles lived with Parker for one year. The bad
times, which were frequent, were greatly overshadowed
by the remarkable amount of musical knowledge he
received from Bird. Parker had great wisdom not only
about music but about survival as well. Unfortunately,
he also had excesses which cost money, much of which
came out of Miles's pocket. His greed stopped there,
because he gave Miles the opportunity to play; and
because he was one of the best players of his time and
mingled with like talent, so did Miles. Parker's association with Gillespie enabled Miles to study with one
of the most gifted trumpeters this country has ever
produced.

Parker prodded Miles for whatever reasons teachers spur their protégés. Miles followed Parker everywhere, and sometimes when Bird was playing a gig he
would be called out to the bandstand to play a few
choruses. Miles developed his confidence very slowly,
and he was always a nervous wreck when Bird beck-
oned to him. He was amazed at Bird's constant progress:

"Bird used to play 40 different styles. He was
never content to remain the same. I remember
how at times he used to turn the rhythm section
around when he and I, Max [Roach], and Duke
Jordan were playing together. Like we'd be play-

13 DeMichael, "Davis," p. 25.
14 Ibid.

ing the blues, and Bird would start on the 11th
bar, and as the rhythm sections stayed where they
were and Bird played where he was, it sounded as
if the rhythm section was on one and three instead
of two and four. Everytime that would happen,
Max used to scream at Duke not to follow Bird
but to stay where he was. Then eventually, it
came around as Bird had planned and we were
together again. Bird used to make me play, try
to play. He used to lead me on the bandstand. I
used to quit every night. The tempo was so up, the
challenge was so great." [15]

That was the revolutionary nature of Bird's music,
always changing to improve, mixing the rhythms and
combining unequal stresses. If one word could describe
the bebop period under Charlie Parker, it would be
"challenging."

Miles has always been aggressive. Even when he
was a kid, if he got the idea to do something he would
try his best to accomplish it. Many point to Miles saying that he was lucky enough to play and record when
he was still developing. Although this is true, it was his
determination that got him to New York and his guts
that made him jump on the bandstand when he had
the chance originally in St. Louis. He made his time
happen. He didn't sit around waiting for it to happen.
It is to his credit that he has been in the recording
studio every year since 1945, an average of three times
each year, either as a sideman or a leader.

He had hardly unpacked his bags in New York
when he received a message that he had been recommended to record in a band led by an alto saxophonist
named Herbie Fields. Fields was an acquaintance of

[15] Nat Hentoff, "Miles," *Down Beat,* November 2, 1955, p. 14.

Parker and had been selected for *Esquire's* New Star
Award on alto in 1945. They were in the studio two
separate times; the band included Lionel Hampton,
Arnett Cobb, and "Slam" Stewart. Hampton played
percussion on the first date and piano on the second.
Most of the music was similar to that which Miles
played in the Randall band, so he really had no problem with it. His problems came when, later that year,
he recorded with Parker. Field's career collapsed late
in the fifties, and, despondent, he committed suicide.

On Parker's first record as a leader he decided to
take Miles, Diz (to play piano), Curly Russell (bass),
and Max Roach (percussion) into the studio. Sadik
Hakim was on hand and he played piano on some of
the takes. Miles always had problems playing Bird's
tricky head lines, and he was so tight on this occasion
that the piece "Ko-Ko" completely threw him, and Diz
had to play his part. On the three pieces he did play
there were a total of twelve takes, and his playing was
a struggle, not brisk or light at all. He obviously was
not ready, and now all the "clinkers" he had played in
public were documented.

In the beginning of 1946 Parker made his ill-
advised trip to Los Angeles, and Miles wasn't very
far behind, touring with the Benny Carter Band. He
found in Carter's band a lyricism he hadn't experienced
previously and began working out ideas that he could
use when he got back with Bird. Parker and Miles
hooked up immediately and were in the recording
studio by March 28th. It was obvious that Bird didn't
like Los Angeles, and the pressure of nonacceptance
everywhere, especially by the critics, began to over-
whelm him. He seemed nervous and irritated in the
studio and mentioned to Miles more than once, his dis-

illusionment with Los Angeles. In the summer, Bird was busted for heroin and committed to Camarillo State Hospital, where he remained for six months.

Miles stayed in Los Angeles for eight months, and, while there, he met Charles Mingus. Mingus had idolized Charlie Parker, so he was eager to meet Parker's protégé. He had saved a little money and wanted to record with Miles and a small band which they had, but the music was never released. Miles grew weary of Los Angeles and was especially uptight when Bird got busted. Then his break came. Fats Navarro quit the Billy Eckstine Orchestra, and Miles entered the band. It was his opportunity to get back to New York. Mingus felt that Miles had an obligation to Parker while he was still in the institution and became furious when Miles decided to return to the East Coast. This hostility between Miles and Mingus has never been resolved; in fact, it has grown deeper over the years. Miles was desperate to get back to New York and just couldn't pass up this opportunity. He knew that Parker would have done the same thing had the situation been reversed. After all, Miles would be right back in the band when Bird returned to New York in the late spring of 1947.

Being in the Eckstine orchestra was like being back home for Miles. This was the first big name band he had worked with; Art Blakey, the percussionist who had made such a big impression on him then, was still there. Blakey, who provided the punch in the band, was one of the prime reasons so many outstanding players wanted to be in it. The Eckstine orchestras of the forties were outstanding organizations which have not received the credit they deserve. Even though they were dance bands centered around Eckstine vocals, Tadd Dameron provided excellent arrangements which allowed for more than adequate expression by the consistently tremendous talents of the band members.

After a short stint with tenorist Illinois Jacquet, Miles returned to the Charlie Parker quintet. He played with more confidence, and it was during this period that he recorded two of his own pieces, "Donna Lee" and "Milestones." Parker had used Miles's lines in the band on numerous occasions before, but this was the first time he saw fit to record one of Miles's compositions. Miles also began organizing his own bands and playing around New York, on several occasions with Sonny Rollins and John Coltrane. All three had played at the Audubon ballroom in Manhattan and had begun a lasting friendship. It was becoming clear that Miles had to find his own way, that his apprenticeship was over. He was still recording with Parker, but his leadership potential had to be realized.

In early 1948, Miles left Parker and played a short time with bassist Oscar Pettiford. He and Bird were to collaborate many times after this, on more equal terms than in the past. Miles had "fronted" one of Parker's albums, but he still hadn't recorded one of his own, and that wasn't going to happen until the end of the year.

In the summer of 1948 Miles started collaborating with Gil Evans and Gerry Mulligan, two former members of the Claude Thornhill band. Their talks produced a small band with unusual voicings, including a French horn and tuba; together, they first made a broadcast from the Royal Roost and then, five months later, the historic recordings with Capitol records. The Royal Roost was a club on Times Square which had been known for its "jazz extravaganzas," and somehow Miles got them to book his "experimental" band for two weeks, an engagement which was supposed to have been its last. Consistent with Miles's fortune up until this time, however, two executives from Capitol records were among the sparse crowd who saw this band. When Miles heard of this, he immediately contacted them, and by January 1949 he was in the Capitol recording studio.

Claude Thornhill's band was a traditional late 1930's dance band that attempted to create a particular sound:

> "Claude had a unique way with a dance band. He'd use the trombones, for instance, with the woodwinds in a way that would give them a horn sound. . . . I think he was the first among pop or jazz bands to evolve that sound. Someone once said, by the way, that Claude was the only man who could play the piano without vibrato. Claude was the first leader to use French horns as a functioning part of a dance band. That distant, haunting, no-vibrato sound came to be blended with the reed and brass sections in various combinations. . . . A characteristic voicing for the Thornhill band was what often happened in ballads. There was a French horn lead, one or sometimes two French horns playing in unison or a duet depending on the character of the melody. The clarinet doubled the melody, also playing the lead. Below were two altos and two tenors. The bottom was normally a double on the melody by baritone or tenor. The reed section sometimes went very low with the saxes being forced to play in a subtone and very soft. In essence, at first, the sound of the band was almost a reduction to an

inactivity of music, to a stillness. Everything—
melody, harmony, rhythm—was moving at mini-
mum speed. . . . Everything was lowered to create a sound, and nothing was to be used to distract
from that sound. The sound hung like a cloud.
But once this stationary effect, this sound, was
created, it was ready to have other things added
to it. The sound itself can only hold interest for a
certain length of time. Then you have to make
certain changes within that sound; you have to
make personal use of harmonies, rather than work
with traditional ones; there has to be more movement in the melody; more dynamics, more syncopation; speeding up of the rhythms. For me, I had
to make those changes. . . . I would say that the
sound was made ready to be used by other forces
in music. I did not create the sound; Claude did.
I did more or less match up with the sound the
different movements by people like Lester, Charlie
and Dizzy in which I was interested. It was their
rhythmic and harmonic revolutions that had influenced me. I liked both aspects and put them together. . . . Those elements were around, looking
for each other." [16]

The principal arranger for the band was Gil Evans.
It was on his premises that Miles produced the Capitol
bands. Ironically, 1948 marked the end of the radio
band and subsequently the dissolution of many dance
bands. While Miles had his band at the Royal Roost,
he was able to broadcast from there quite frequently.
It is a paradox that this mechanism which almost put
an end to the dance band era became a vanguard for
one of that era's leading arrangers. Gil Evans' music

[16] Gil Evans in Wilfred Mellers, *Music in A New Found Land*
(London: Barrie and Rockliff, 1964), pp. 354–355.

had a tremendous influence on Miles's music, and, in turn, Miles's concepts of rhythms and his lyrical playing style in general affected Evans. Over a period of fourteen years (1948 to 1962), they collaborated on five or six albums, played for television, and performed at Carnegie Hall. As Charlie Parker had been Miles's teacher, so Evans provided the structure through which Miles saw himself expanding the orchestrative concepts of bebop. With Parker there was never a rehearsal; oddly enough, he and Miles rarely talked about music, everything was so spontaneous. Conversely, the Capitol band rehearsed, planned, knew exactly what it wanted to do, and did it.

There were three separate recording sessions, two in 1949 and one in 1950, after Miles returned from his first trip to Paris. The first date, January 21, 1949, produced the following: "Jeru," a Gerry Mulligan piece, arranged by himself; "Godchild," a George Wallington composition arranged by Mulligan; "Budo," by Bud Powell and Miles, arranged by pianist John Lewis; and "Move," by Denzil Best and arranged by Lewis. The April 22, 1949, meeting produced "Boplicity" by Miles, arranged by Gil Evans, "Venus De Milo" by Mulligan, "Rouge" by John Lewis, and "Israel" by John Carisi, each arranged by its composer. The last session, March 9, 1950, offered "Deception," composed and arranged by Miles, "Rocker," written and arranged by Mulligan, "Darn That Dream," written by James Van Heusen and arranged by Mulligan, and an arrangement by Gil Evans of Chummy MacGregor's "Moon Dreams."

Even though the plans and executions of this music stretched over a two-year period, there was amazing continuity to all three sessions. The total playing time was thirty-one minutes and thirty-five seconds, much of which was taken up by the complex arrangements. Usually the improvisations were no more than two choruses, and almost all were strongly supported by the band playing very strong, rich, active harmonies. The personnel remained essentially the same, with Miles, Lee Konitz (alto sax), Gerry Mulligan (baritone sax), and Bill Barber (tuba) playing all three dates. Max Roach (drums) played the first and third dates, with Kenny Clarke in the middle one, Al Haig was on piano during the first session, and John Lewis played for the second and third. The bassists and French horn players changed with each session; Joe Shulman (1), Nelson Boyd (2) and Al McKibbon (3) on bass, and Junior Collins (1), Sandy Siegelstein (2), and Gunther Schuller (3) on French horn. The trombone chair was also shared, Kai Winding doing the first session and J. J. Johnson doing the second and third. There was no guitar, although it had gained substantial importance in the swing bands. Much of the accompaniment was done by the full band playing chords like a piano. The consistency of the recordings was largely due to the fact that much of the music was written.

The reintroduction of the tuba, in some cases used as a melodic instrument, allowed the music to emanate from the bass clef up into the higher voices. "Godchild" began with the baritone sax playing the melodic line in unison with the tuba, which played it an octave lower. The last phrases are passed through a series of sequences to the higher voices, giving the piece a feeling of evolution. "Jeru" started low and moved, similarly to "Godchild," up through the voices. The tuba played the melodic line but again supported the melody an octave lower. Instead of working toward brilliant timbre, this band played a muted sound, preferring to exploit the lower half of instrument timbre. What resulted was an even balance of sound through the use of the total range of the instruments involved. Thus, the tuba changed from just an instrument on which to punch out redundant bass lines to another voice in the spectrum.

This was not the first time that the lower part of a band was explored. Ellington was one of the first composer/arrangers to investigate the possibilities of deeper timbre, through baritone saxophonist Harry Carney. Even though Mulligan, Konitz, and Evans had recently played in the Thornhill band, their inspiration came from Ellington and his principal arranger, Billy Strayhorn. Miles gave much credit to Ellington for providing the initial format on which to expand.

The improvisations of the Capitol sessions were the weakest aspects of the music, taking a subordinate role to the arrangements. Besides Miles, whose work will be discussed later, Lee Konitz and Gerry Mulligan shared the bulk of the soloing, although Kai Winding, J. J. Johnson, John Lewis, Kenny Clarke, and Max Roach made token contributions. Konitz's sound was very thin and he moved through most of his solos unconfidently. His articulation was not always clear, sliding to a note instead of hitting it. Mulligan was generally adequate, but in the higher register of the baritone, he, too, sounded thin and unsure. There was a lot of apprehension about this music because of the fact that it was, harmonically, very advanced. Certainly one of the unfortunate effects of this trend was the move away from improvisation which precipitated the so-called "cool" period.

In addition to the advanced ideas about harmonies and their movements, the sessions made significant con-

tributions to the realm of melody. "Israel" was one of
the many examples in this collection which was shaped
in the tradition of bebop. It began with a short, four-
bar introduction leading into a twelve-bar jumping,
jagged melodic line; its definite A-A'-B form produced
a strong feeling of call-and-response, although it was
the most non-lyrical of all the pieces. It was an instru-
mental piece; bebop traditionally emphasized instru-
mental style. There was, especially in the solo playing,
a strong influence of Lester Young. His influence even
reached the syncopation of the pieces; time after time,
they interchanged strong and weak accents. All of the
compositions, with the exception of "Moon Dreams"
and "Darn That Dream," the two pieces not written
by any of the participants, bear the heavy stamp of
bebop.

For this literate music, the band was built on
musicians who were strong readers. It did launch a
line of other bands whose intent was to play complicated written lines rather than spontaneous improvisations, but what Miles himself was trying to do in this
band was to perform amidst a sound. He heard that
sound coming out of the bass clef into the treble, only
occasionally above the grand staff. He heard his own
voice there, and since it had been made clear to him
earlier by Gillespie that he couldn't hear in the higher
register, he knew he had better exploit the middle. The
consequence of all this was a long line of imitators who
were not really interested in improvisational music, but
rather needed a mechanism to exploit African-American
music. The so-called "cool" period cropped up to give
"jazz" its unemotional, literate guise. While all this was
happening, Miles's career took a nose dive, equaled only
by the 1929 stock market crash. Gil Evans became ob-

scure, partially because of a decline in interest in dance bands, but in 1957 he emerged again with Miles. On the other hand, Gerry Mulligan and Lee Konitz soared in popularity from this period.

During the whole time between 1948 and 1950 Miles was in and out of the Tadd Dameron band. The musical evolution of Miles cannot be clearly understood if it isn't seen in context with Dameron. Miles first knew him in St. Louis when Tadd was in the Eckstine orchestra and was its principal arranger. Miles played in Tadd's best-known band, the one which existed from 1948 until 1950. They played at the Royal Roost, where, most likely, it was Tadd who was responsible for getting Miles's experimental band heard. Dameron played his first professional gigs with trumpeter Freddie Webster, also one of Miles's early influences. During the forties Tadd became known as one of the few arrangers who had a clear understanding of bebop and its challenging, revolutionary processes. Dameron assisted in the formulation of many of the ideas that Miles brought to his experimental band. His piano style, although much more fluid, was very similar to Thelonius Monk's, especially in many of his turning phrases.

Between his second and third sessions with Capitol, Miles made his first trip to Paris, to play in the 1949 Paris Jazz Festival. He had played in the Metronome All-Star Band in January and was becoming somewhat established. Also, he and Tadd had broadcast from the Roost, and the Jazz Festival seemed ripe for the picking. However, he found himself bored in Paris. France was really a foreign country to him as he sat around and, for the first time in his life, waited for things to happen. Being around Parker for so long, he had naturally become acquainted with drugs, but because he was learning about the business and trying to keep up with the discipline of learning about music, he kept fairly clean. Unfortunately, the boredom in Paris led him into serious trouble with drugs. He came back from Europe in the summer, while Dameron went to England to arrange for the Ted Heath band.

Miles was now added to the long list of forties and fifties musicians who became junkies, mainly due to the accessibility of the stuff. Now his fortune changed radically, and he played in an assortment of bands around New York, some led by himself and others with his contemporaries, Sonny Rollins, J. J. Johnson, and Lee Konitz. He continued making records, but his out-of-town gigs were solo with local rhythm sections backing him up, which is always a drag. On one trip he made to Pittsburgh, he worked at a bar which closed down before he even got paid. It was only with the help of a local friend that he was able to get back to New York. He had all the rationalizations that most heavy drug users have for that suicide trip: he believed his music sounded better, that his consciousness had reached a new level. What really happened was that his health deteriorated, and, had he continued, he would have met the cruel fate of Jimmy Blanton, Charlie Christian, and Fats Navarro.

Filling Navarro's chair in the Dameron band, Miles was succeeding him for the second time; Fats had sat in the first trumpet chair, with Diz second and Miles third, in the 1948–49 Metronome All-Stars, in which position he was direct predecessor to Clifford Brown. Regrettably, Navarro became hopelessly addicted in the mid-forties and, in the last year before he died (1950), was practically incapacitated. A drastic weight loss caused numerous weaknesses, until he contracted pneumonia. Navarro had an outstanding technique of maneuverability which allowed him to turn on a dime and hit hard intervals. He had total control of all registers and played everything with directness. The music of bebop featured staccato, and even though its leader, Parker, was a saxophonist, it was perfect for the trumpet. Diz, Miles, Fats, Clifford Brown, and hard bop players Kenny Dorham, Lee Morgan, Donald Byrd, Freddie Hubbard, and Booker Little all took to bop with its progressions ad infinitum. Navarro's short career inevitably stirs gross speculation about his potential and his contribution, but he was an influential player in his time. Every one of the above trumpeters was motivated in some way by Navarro.

These were hard times for Miles, so he didn't play out of New York too often; yet he kept his name before the public through his recordings and radio broadcasts. Between the summer of 1949 and the summer of 1953, he had nineteen recording dates, including the last session at Capitol, nine radio broadcasts (live from Birdland), and a concert at Carnegie Hall. He made the 1950–51 Metronome All-Star Band probably on the strength of his Capitol sessions. Though only he and Max Roach were black, the other All-Star players were also associated with those historic recordings. This was perhaps the most physically trying period for him, but it was a strong "woodshedding" time in which Miles would record his transition from a mediocre, but creative, musician to a brilliant one. Neither John Coltrane nor Charlie Parker had had that opportunity, but hearing Trane's musical transition in person was inspiring to Miles. That unquenchable aspiration alone attests to Miles's aggressiveness and his ability to survive.

Miles recorded mostly with his peers. In all of the

air time mentioned, Parker appeared only twice and Diz once. Sonny Rollins, J. J. Johnson, John Lewis, Max Roach, Roy Haynes, Percy Heath, Gil Goggins, Art Blakey, and a young alto saxophonist named Jackie McLean, who got his first date with Miles, were the black brothers who were now being encouraged by Miles, finding a forum for their music. Miles was out front in creativity and recognition but he was closely followed by the young Clifford Brown. Brown, who was "discovered" by Dameron, was the only trumpeter of the fifties who was in no way influenced by Miles. He was in direct line with Navarro, using flawless techniques in all registers, unique ability to turn and leap through all registers, plus a stylized sound which quickly twisted and bent notes to give the music some lyricism. Clifford was an excellent composer whose lines generally followed the pattern set by bebop, but added a strong song quality to them. They were more singable than most of the jumping lines the forties produced. Clifford made another substantial contribution to the music through his unusual character: he neither smoked nor drank and was almost totally clean. But in 1950, Brown was hospitalized for a year by an auto accident; in 1956, he was killed in another accident on the Pennsylvania Turnpike. Unquestionably, he was changing the course of the music; had he lived, he probably would have been one of the finest improvisers this music has ever known.

It seems more than just an accident of history that Miles should dramatically walk into Baker's Keyboard Lounge in Detroit with the Max Roach/Clifford Brown quintet performing and begin playing "My Funny Valentine." This was early in 1954, and Miles was playing single with a local rhythm section at the Bluebird

Bar, not far from Baker's. Drugs had now taken their
toll and pushed him near the point of no return. That
night, he suddenly walked into the lounge where his
competitor group was playing, interrupted the band
with his own rendition of his favorite ballad, and
walked out.

Soon after this, he kicked the addiction. In an interview, Miles reflects:

> "I made up my mind I was getting off dope,"
> he said. "I was sick and tired of it. You know you
> can get tired of anything. You can even get tired
> of being scared. I laid down and stared at the
> ceiling for 12 days, and I cursed everybody I didn't
> like. I was kicking it the hard way. It was like
> having a bad case of flu, only worse. I threw up
> everything I tried to eat. My pores opened up and
> I smelled like chicken soup. Then it was over." [17]

Miles gives the impression that he's the only one
who has ever had a "jones"; nevertheless, kicking heroin
is a mighty feat. He learned how to exploit himself
positively in this situation, and he capitalized on the
lesson later, in the middle and late fifties.

He did most of his recording during the early part
of the fifties with Blue Note Record Company and,
then, Prestige Records. It was at the end of the Blue
Note period that he really began to blossom. Beginning
with his recording date of March 6, 1954, almost ten
months after his last recording and nine months from
his last broadcast, a new confidence sprang into his
music. (This was also right after the Detroit episode.)
He first worked with a quartet including Horace Silver
(piano), Percy Heath (bass), and Art Blakey (percus-

17 DeMichael, "Davis," p. 25.

sion). They made two solid dates, with Heath and Silver especially crisp and ready to play. Percy's playing with Miles, in a period that lasted over a year, covering six recording dates, clearly showed his consistency and his imaginative accompaniment. His intonation was remarkable, especially because the bass, among Western classical instruments, is probably the hardest to keep in tune. Heath was among the most brilliant bassists of the fifties, always keeping tempo like a heartbeat, with excellent note selection. Even among the many exciting bass players who appeared in the fifties, Heath was still outstanding.

The quality of Silver's solo work has never caught up with that of his accompaniment, which is as accomplished as this music has ever known. Bebop, with its total exploitation of European harmonic music, created a whole series of remarkable accompanists, beginning with Tadd Dameron and Bud Powell, followed by hard bop's John Lewis, "Red" Garland, and Sonny Clark; unquestionably, Horace was the icing on the cake. On any given set of chord progressions, for any piece, he would play inversions, alternates, exchanges of major and minor scales, and half-steps moving to the dominant chord, all with perfect anticipation, always swinging. He was especially potent on up-tempo numbers, where his accompaniment would pounce on the soloist. Combined with the inspiration that Miles brought to the recording dates, Silver was unbeatable.

Art Blakey was certainly more than adequate for these sessions, but Miles usually played with a different kind of drummer. Studying Miles's choices, starting with Max Roach, a quintet/quartet percussionist with a melodic concept of duration, then Kenny Clarke, "Philly" Joe Jones, Art Taylor, Jimmy Cobbs, Tony Williams and Jack DeJohnette, one sees that the similarity in their approach lies in using multidirectional rhythms.

There is some change in the dimension of a musician when he has turned the corner and is heading straight out; he becomes definite about the people he chooses to work with. Miles did so, regarding every recording as a document of his music. These sessions propelled Miles, and, even though he couldn't afford to have a full-time band, he always made sure his associates were together when he recorded. He became known as a musician's musician around New York, although he was still relatively unknown outside of the "Apple." He took advantage of the fact that he had more control over his material and fellow players when he recorded, especially when he moved to Prestige. All these circumstances helped create the historic recording of "Walkin'" on April 29, 1954.

Soon after, on June 29, he recorded again, keeping the same rhythm section but changing the horns. The session was with Rollins playing three of his own pieces, "Airegin," "Oleo," and "Doxy." Only in his mid-twenties, Rollins had already contributed three compositions that were to become "jazz standards." His playing here was strong but with a few shrieks that have haunted him all his career. But the most definitive music of this era was produced in the "Walkin'" session, which included J. J. Johnson, Lucky Thompson (tenor sax), Silver, Heath, and Kenny Clarke. The two pieces they recorded were among the longest in terms of improvised time up until then. Miles had first met Thompson in the 1944 Eckstine band, and they locked up again in Los Angeles playing in Mingus' band. Thompson was the personification of the "light and under" sound, although he had a big vibrato; his playing fa-

vored Don Byas and Lester Young. This was to be one
of his last recordings before going to Europe, more or
less permanently. He never attained prominence, even
after he won some of the popularity awards in the late
forties, but his playing here was strong with an excellent, round tone. Where J. J. and Miles played on
the beat, Thompson lagged slightly behind, connecting
phrases with an incredible sense of duration.

The recordings of "Blue 'n' Boogie" and "Walkin' "
by this sextet established Miles as the leading voice of
the music. It was total musical concentration that combined and fused to produce the finest recording of the
first five years of the fifties; the reason was not a single
person or factor, because there were six people who
all contributed equally well. The rhythm was superb.
Heath and Silver were so consistent; Percy accompanied Miles with such a great tempo, always on the
mark, with a skip now and then, but always there with
prodigious intonation. When bebop gave the line to the
bass, it gave it to Percy Heath. His steady lines allowed
Silver to be even more inventive in his accompaniment,
since he knew that the pulse and progression would be
there. Heath was one of the first bassists on whom Miles
asked the piano to lay out, just so he could play with
only the other line and percussion. Miles even found
himself standing between the bass and drums during
his public appearances.

The three horns on "Walkin'," which was named
after the pace the bass line developed during the bop
period, played excellent traditional blues in twelve-bar
form, mostly in medium tempo, giving a classic treatment of hard bop. Miles began his improvisations lagging slightly behind the beat, then on it, then to
double-time, finishing right on the beat. Johnson, with

his flawless technique, played mostly in the lower register, sliding to and bouncing out of it, always playing the right combination of accents in his melodic phrases. Thompson was bellowing, juxtaposing triads, staying mostly behind the beat with that big, round vibrato tone. If hard bop could be classified as the classic era of jazz in which the new innovations of bebop were applied to traditional forms like the twelve- and sixteen-bar blues, then this session, along with the 1959 Town Hall concert by Thelonius Monk, was definitely the high-water mark.

In the mid-fifties the music began to move farther downtown in New York. Greenwich Village opened several bars expressly for jazz. Miles was still without a steady band, but was working frequently with his early fifties associates and recording when he thought the time was right. On Christmas Eve of 1954, he gathered together three-quarters of the Modern Jazz Quartet (Heath, Clarke, and Milt Jackson) and Thelonius Monk for a date at Prestige. It was an unusual session, since Miles had never recorded with Monk before and was unsure of how it would turn out. They recorded four pieces, Milt Jackson's "Bags' Groove," Denzil Best's "Bemsha Swing," Miles's "Swing Spring," and the standard Gershwin tune "The Man I Love." The mood of all the recording was melancholy. There were two takes each of "Bags'" and "Love," all of which were issued. Monk did very little accompanying, most of that coming from Jackson and Heath. During one of the cuts of "The Man I Love," Monk actually stopped playing during his solo for almost a whole chorus, finally resuming when Miles played a few bars to get him back on the track. Miles, during his improvisations on this same piece, stopped to squeeze the mute into the trumpet (which can be heard on the record) and continued. In spite of these distractions, the music was truly spectacular. Miles established himself as one of the outstanding ballad players of this or any time period. Jackson and Heath, who by this time had allowed themselves to get bogged down in the controlled music of the Modern Jazz Quartet, seemed to burst forth in this surprisingly loose structure. Percy again penetrated the very soul of this session. He never lost a beat, and his pulse was right on top, even through all the distractions.

Monk was whatever Monk is. He has always been faulted for his questionable technique, but even if he had the most "dangerous" technique on the planet he would still play the same way. He has moved very little from the first time he started playing as a professional, yet what he plays he does so well that he's never been copied. The humor that periodically crops up in his music, as in his playing part of "How Dry I Am" during his improvisation on "The Man I Love," only disguises the genius of the subtle but sophisticated rhythm structures he develops. These structures show up clearly in his compositions "Friday the Thirteenth," "Little Rootie Tootie," "Trinkle Tinkle," "Criss-Cross" and "Straight, No Chaser." They demonstrate his keen insight into pulse and accents. Monk has often been observed moving his legs at a different tempo, time or rhythm from the piece being played. This idiosyncrasy illustrates his ability to hear multiple rhythms and all their possibilities.

These sessions of 1954 marked a definite upsurge for Miles as a musician. Though he was unable to support a band until the end of 1955, he used these sessions to search for the size and instrumentation of that band.

It was both economically unfeasible and illogical to select his most recent collaborators for his new band. They represent strong leadership themselves and would eventually have their own bands or would be essential parts of others. He worked quite frequently, mostly with the above people, but also with new arrivals Philly Joe Jones (percussion) and Red Garland (piano).

In the middle of 1955 Miles received an invitation from Charlie Mingus to record for Mingus' small record outfit, Debut. In retrospect, it seems to have been rank individualism that kept these two gifted musicians from working together more often than they have over the years. This one date they did make was a strong indication of the musical connection they were into. The session was in jeopardy when Miles hadn't showed an hour and a half after the recording was supposed to have begun, but he finally made it, claiming that he had been waiting for someone from Debut to pick him up. Mingus was irate but held his composure, and the proceedings began. Since this was actually Mingus' date with Miles leading it, the personnel were all in Mingus' band at that time. Elvin Jones, who had just arrived from Detroit, was on percussion. The vibes player was Teddy Charles, with trombonist Britt Woodman, and Mingus on bass.

They recorded four pieces, all unusual standards: "Nature Boy," "Alone Together," "There Is No You," and "Easy Living." It was a long session because Miles played further and further away from the progressions, and it seemed as if they were constantly starting over. But none of this shows up in the music, which was excellent. Mingus' arrangements were stellar and did nothing but enhance Miles's style. All the numbers were in the same rather slow tempo with the exception of "There Is No You." Woodman, Mingus, Charles, and Miles provided spellbinding interpretations through their improvisations. Woodman was especially effective not only as a soloist but most essentially as an accompanist for Miles. Whether or not the lines were written or improvised by him, they were stunning both in support of Miles and as a contrast to him.

"Alone Together" began with a short introduction, after which Miles took the line with Woodman ornamenting around it. In the middle of a phrase, Woodman took up the line while Miles played the ornamentation, done so smoothly that one can hardly hear the exchange; even the timbre was so close that only Woodman's vibrato gave the exchange away. Woodman was haunting behind Miles, playing active notes, minor and diminished passing tones. Mingus, never content with playing the pulse, was skipping, double-timing, adding a third line. Charles played chords behind the soloists and interesting lines, especially next to the trombone. Mingus played topping solos, striking glissandos with his fingers, constantly dialoguing with the instrument. He moved the pieces with his inventive arrangements, especially when he changed tempos and rhythms. And as in "Birth of the Cool," there seemed to be a great emphasis on creating a sound.

No one understood better than Miles what being invited to play at Newport could mean to one's career, so he jumped at the chance in 1955, even though he was a last-minute addition. He was magnanimous, playing alongside Zoot Sims, Gerry Mulligan, Thelonious Monk, Percy Heath and Connie Kay. The critics made a find and Miles was catapulted into national "jazz" prominence, although he played on only two numbers, "Hackensack," Monk's composition, and "Now's the

Time" by Parker. He was sandwiched in between a small band led by Basie and the Dave Brubeck group on the last night, an obvious appeasement of the "modernists" of that time. His playing was so strong that he was noticed by every critic who covered the festival. In fact, they all mentioned him positively in their columns. At the time he recorded the Debut date (July 9) he hadn't even heard he would be on the Newport bill at all. Now he was being mentioned as the possible leader of a pickup band there. That's how strongly he demonstrated leadership and outstanding musicianship.

The night before Miles's celebrated appearance, Clifford Brown had brought down the house in his band with Max Roach. Interestingly enough, no one made comparisons between Brown and Miles in the review columns, probably because Miles was still just some obscure trumpet player who once worked with Charlie Parker. Brown held the reins, and no one had challenged him. He was as alone in the fifties as "Trane" was in the sixties. In this festival band, which also included Richie Powell (piano), Harold Land (tenor sax), and George Morrow (bass), Brown played bebop at its utmost, expanding its every aspect. If his crash death hadn't come in 1956, he might have played with Coltrane, since even then he was certainly penetrating through the harmonic system. At this second Newport Jazz Festival, Miles was respected and admired by his contemporaries but virtually unknown outside of the New York cadre.

Within a month Miles was again in the recording studio, this time with the young alto player Jackie McLean, who had played alto with him once before. This would be his last experiment before almost ex-

clusively using the tenor saxophone plus rhythm. Milt
Jackson and the rhythm of Ray Bryant (piano), Percy
Heath, and Arthur Taylor (percussion) rounded out the
band.

Ironically, Sonny Rollins was Miles's final choice
as the other horn player in the band, but he was out
of town when Miles heard about the date from Columbia. So Miles temporarily used a Philadelphian,
John Coltrane, whom he had known in the late forties
when Trane first came to New York with Cal Massey.
Even then, Miles occasionally played gigs with both
Sonny and Trane. As one would surmise from all of
Miles's activities, he would never pick a stranger to
occupy an important sideman role on a recording date.
He had worked with Garland and Jones previously, but
Paul Chambers, the twenty-year-old bassist who had
come to New York from Detroit with Donald Byrd,
was the surprise selection. Jackie McLean had first
mentioned Chambers to Miles when he and Paul had
played together in the George Wallington Quintet. This
was the same group that recorded live at the Café
Bohemia, helping to perpetuate the growing interest in
jazz in Greenwich Village. Miles, showing his ability to
pick extraordinary talent, kept Chambers as his bassist
almost exclusively for the next seven years. Chambers
was one of the first bass players to combine arco and
pizzicato equally in his solo work. His arco style was
reminiscent of "Slam" Stewart, who sang when he
played with a bow, occasionally at a third or fifth away.
Miles loved to "walk" (trumpet, bass, and percussion
in a walking tempo) with Chambers, who always knew
the exact time to double-time, skip, or pounce on the
note. He was the perfect accompanist for Miles.

This was the first of Miles's many great rhythm

sections, which included Red Garland, Chambers and Philly Joe Jones. Jones fired up the whole band every night as he and Trane baffled critics with their apparent bludgeoning of the music; he used every limb to propel the music and drove Trane to the edge of infinity. Philly Joe was quick, smooth, and sometimes bombastic. He greatly influenced Trane's sixties percussionist Elvin Jones.

Too much publicity has been given to the fact that Red Garland had once been a fighter, implying that was the reason why Miles hired him. True, Miles is a longtime admirer of boxing (he once thought of doing it himself), but he hired him because he realized that Garland was a most inventive pianist. His block chording fit Miles's concepts of harmony, always maintaining a wide harmonic range. His interlocking chord structures produced interesting inside voicings; his rhythms were outstanding as well, which ability links him with McCoy Tyner.

Paul Chambers was the only member of this early band who was retained for a long period of time after the early fall of 1955. Miles frequently changed piano players and percussionists; Tommy Flanagan and Tadd Dameron handled the piano and Art Taylor saw a lot of action as percussionist. When Sonny Rollins returned from a half-year stay in Chicago, he immediately stepped into the band but then dropped out when he received the call from Max Roach and Clifford Brown to play in their band. Trane was in Miles's band now and the combination of the two with Paul, Red and Philly Joe dashed out music like an endless fountain of fresh ideas and created the most consistently progressing group of the next four years. This band was not completely formulated until the middle of 1956 when Miles, trying to fulfill his obligations with Prestige, recorded twelve pieces without doing one extra take. It took a particularly strong and subtle leadership to forge together all the energy that this band could tap, and Miles provided that leadership.

Sometime between the time of his initial contact with Columbia Records in 1955 and the summer of 1956 when he completed his first album for that company, Miles underwent a minor throat operation, after which he could not speak above a whisper if he wanted to use his full voice again. Although Columbia was his breakthrough, he still had commitments to Prestige, and it was in an ensuing argument about these commitments that Miles raised his voice, causing irreparable damage to his vocal cords. Though he had to whisper for only a few weeks, Miles couldn't keep his voice down. His need to liberate himself from an exploitative situation precipitated the quarrel. Although his voice became gravelly and slightly above a whisper, it didn't affect his playing. They settled on two more recording sessions.

This uncompromising spirit increased his stock among the people and helped to create the twelve-piece performance on May 11, 1956, and still another, again with twelve, on October 26, all without a single retake. These were his final recordings for Prestige, leaving them a legacy that they issued over sixteen years and at least seven albums, including reissues. These takes are a testimony to Miles's leadership qualities and, considering the diversity of the collective pieces, the flexibility of the quintet. The compositions included Rollins' "Oleo" and "Airegin," the old bepop tune "Salt Peanuts" by Kenny Clarke, unfamiliar standards like "Diane," "The Surrey With the Fringe on

Top," "If I Were a Bell," "You're My Everything," and jazz standards "Woody'n You," Gillespie's tune, and Monk's "Well You Needn't." Miles added what has now become his most famous ballad, "My Funny Valentine," a hodgepodge of pieces all treated in that aggressive, straightforward style that hallmarked this band. Philly Joe motivated Miles to stand between the percussionist and double bass player when he was improvising. Trane was always looking over Garland's shoulder to follow the progressions, but he was also transfixed by the artistry of Jones. In fact, Trane favored Philly Joe so much that he chose Elvin Jones, who had paid considerable attention to Philly Joe, as his first and longtime percussionist.

Paul Chambers was setting a standard of double bass playing that would not be easily matched. He was a giant because he knew what he could do with the instrument and did it, dexterously fretting in all the positions on all four strings, equally strong near the bridge as at the neck. He wasn't as strong a pulse bassist as Percy Heath, but who was? Although he lost the progressions on "My Funny Valentine" when Garland was playing his solo, he recovered nicely and generally he was fluent in harmonic movement. Considering the transient status of most practitioners of African-American music, Chambers' seven-year tenure with Miles was a particularly long one. It was, in part, his accompaniment that helped Miles's career soar, accompaniments such as the piano layout on "Airegin" or all of "When Lights Are Low" or the beginning of "If I Were a Bell," all recorded on October 26, 1956, when Paul was only twenty-one.

Though a comparison of Miles and Trane in these sessions may arouse controversy, Miles certainly was more mature and relaxed in his playing. Trane was still groping, playing phrases that were incomplete, pushing instead of approaching the music with more confidence; there were moments on several of the pieces that he would stop playing in order to see what progressions Garland was playing and. how they were connecting. Miles, on the other hand, was assertive, responding to his accompaniment with great assurance, especially on some of the more banal pieces. The time between 1955 and 1960 might have been Miles's most productive period. It was a time when aesthetic African-American music was meandering into disjunct patterns; when, after the deaths of Charlie Parker and Clifford Brown, Max Roach and Sonny Rollins experimented with ¾ time, there was nothing in the history or the tradition of the music that would indicate ternary forms. Also created between '55 and '60 was a nebulous thing called "third stream music," advocated by Gunther Schuller and John Lewis; it was forced "marriage" between European classical techniques and African-American music. During this most confused period, Miles employed the most dynamic rhythm section around *and* a tenor saxophone sideman who was probably the most gifted musician this country has ever produced in any idiom. And Miles's own music showed steady progress.

Contrary to general belief, the personnel in his bands from 1955 to 1957 changed considerably. Miles was still hiring himself out as a single if the pie was sweet enough, but, in spite of his Newport success, he still wasn't able to maintain a full-time band for anywhere near fifty-two weeks a year. But when he was recording, he used the same quintet each time he went into the studio. After a short time, Miles was able to support a band for more than a half year and made the

above personnel plus "Cannonball" Adderley an unusual offer.

Between the May 11 and October 26 dates Miles
played the flügelhorn for the first time in public. He
had been into the horn for quite some time but hadn't
had the occasion to use it until he received a call to
participate in a unique ensemble for brass and rhythm
section. Incidentally, this was an independent effort,
recorded by Columbia, of which only a thousand copies
were issued; the importance of this event has been
cloaked because of the unavailability of information
about it. There were two sessions, the first on Saturday,
October 20, and the second on October 23. The album
was called *Music for Brass*, and it contained original
pieces by J. J. Johnson, John Lewis, and Jimmy Giuffre.
Miles played on two of the takes, "Three Little Feelings" and "Poem for Brass." But more interesting and
important are the circumstances surrounding Miles's
being there at all. Miles had had his first experience in
the Columbia studios in the fall of 1955, recording two
pieces. Still committed to Prestige, he didn't return to
Columbia until June, 1956, finishing the takes for his
first album and doing a "promo" for Columbia's *The
Story of Jazz* narrated by Leonard Bernstein. He had
heard about the brass date from J. J. and, while doing
the promo, he was invited to participate. Ironically,
Miles had seen the music previously and had been interested for some time in being involved with the project, but he waited until he was asked rather than
volunteering himself. Although rather reticent when he
was first with Parker, Miles now saw his worth and
musicianship and began to command respect from all
sectors of his public. The image that had been developing for years was now at full acceleration and Miles

would seek out no longer. He was not an entertainer, he was an artist, and those who had misjudged the music he represented misjudged him. The throat operation allowed him to be more introverted and direct, while the critics gave him a personality to exploit.

Music for Brass was a windfall for Miles. He gleaned from it possibilities for expanding his 1948 experimental band. The concept of just brass showed him colors which could be adapted from the brass, his major instrument group. Lines connected up through the range of brass instruments, moving, almost hocket in style, among the voices. This captured Miles's concentration, and soon he and Gil Evans got down to work. The flügelhorn is a natural instrument for Miles, because its lower sonority seems to be in the range that he hears best. The horn itself is a valve bugle, usually in B♭ and like the bugle except that it has a chromatic range down to F♯ below middle C. It's an awkward instrument because of its bulk, but it has a thick, mellow timbre. Interestingly enough, Clark Terry has used the instrument extensively and was one of the first persons to acquaint Miles with it. Within a year, Miles put his own large band together and, along with Gil Evans' arrangements, used the flügelhorn exclusively.

On his first trip to Paris in 1949, Miles had established himself firmly in the minds of people who organize concerts and are general patrons of the arts. France was a good place to relax, so, shortly after his last trip into the Prestige studio, he went to Paris to think about his next music project and to play occasionally. Actually he had a gig when he went over, playing in a concert in Zurich, Switzerland, with a French trio of Rene Urtreger (piano), Pierre Michelot (bass), and Christian Garros (percussion). One of Miles's favorite

European classical composers has been Debussy, and his music for large bands reflects the colors of this European Impressionist. On this second trip Miles hung out with André Hodeir, the French musicologist who had written a book about Debussy. He also met Michel Legrande, the French composer/arranger whose music is highly influenced by Debussy also. These three talked about the *Music for Brass* album and the ideas Miles and Gil Evans were putting together. Hodeir had just completed his book *Jazz: Its Evolution and Essence* and was anxious to get Miles's impression. He declined the invitation, although this was one of the first music books to give him a serious play. There are long descriptions of the Capitol bands and Hodeir's writings indicate a deep admiration for Miles's music. This admiration began when Miles first showed Hodeir the music in 1949. Before he left France Miles agreed to return and do the score for the film *Ascenseur Pour l'Echafaud* by Louis Mallé.

The brass dates had paralyzed Miles and consumed his musical thoughts. Before leaving for Paris he had disbanded his quintet, so when he returned to New York he worked with a variety of personnel, including tenor saxophonist Bobby Jasper, whom he had met in Europe, and Sonny Rollins. Tommy Flanagan (piano) and Art Taylor also entered and exited occasionally, but, speaking frankly of where he was in 1957, Miles was experiencing transition, so he tried all the best musicians around New York but settled only on Paul Chambers. He made two albums that year, one a musically unsuccessful scoring for a film and the other, *Miles Ahead* for Columbia.

Comparing the personnel and instrumentation of Miles's first large orchestra (for the Capitol sessions) with the *Music for Brass* contingency, there are some striking resemblances, though the late forties unit was really a chamber orchestra. The *Brass* band had one less trumpet, the same number of trombones, one less French horn, no bass trombone, one alto sax, a bass clarinet, two flutes, one clarinet, no baritone horns, bass and percussion; no piano was used in either band. The sound of both bands is bright, but Miles's earlier group sings more and seems generally more on the mark. With Gil Evans arranging and directing, the band replaces the piano as an accompaniment; Miles is the only soloist here, whereas on *Brass,* Joe Wilder solos and does a dynamic job. Eric Dolphy's arranging for Coltrane's "Africa" is a masterpiece; I can't recall an arranger who was able to fit the pieces so well together when combining Miles with a large instrument. More than anything, Evans understood Miles's chromaticism. Miles is most effective when he can play a series of short rhythmic phrases, so Evans doesn't just fill in the spaces, he provides a steady flow for Miles to lie on, weave through, and emerge from. Their next two collaborations, *Porgy and Bess* and *Sketches of Spain,* have essentially the same instrument color, except a harp is added in the latter; neither used the piano.

The strongest aspect of *Miles Ahead,* which took four dates to complete, is that even though there are ten different pieces written by eight different composers, it sounds like a suite. There is a great unity of sound throughout, with each piece being connected by harmonic progressions, some elaborate, some with only one active chord. The music is essentially in the lower registers, so when the lines do move to the higher registers, they usually move dramatically, but it is never done loudly. Using mutes and other accessories, the band plays these difficult arrangements relaxed and controlled. Evans' conducting of these sessions is a credit to his knowledge of how to integrate a piece of music. The beautiful "My Ship," by Kurt Weill, is introduced by bass clarinet, trombones, and French horns which literally sing the piece. When arrangements like these are articulated as cleanly as this band can, an artistic work emerges which still sounds interesting years later.

There are so many colors in this music because its pace is constant but multidirectional and syncopated. Chambers and Taylor are handling the rhythm, both doing more than asked. Chambers' task of playing many written parts and others with only assigned changes is especially effective. He plays many sequences with the tuba which are moving in opposite directions, handling them flawlessly in excellent intonation. He obviously studied the music earlier, because there are many abrupt tempo changes, rhythm changes, and free rhythm parts occurring at the beginning, middle, and end of phrases, all of which he negotiates impeccably. Percussionists for big bands have certain responsibilities which restrict their freedom somewhat, but Taylor manages to push this band and still be very sensitive to what the music demands. The accompanying job Evans does for Miles is superb, making this an important document of their unusually fine musical understanding.

Miles, having developed to a certain pivotal point, could now realize his artistic visions; with this orchestra, Miles was able to create a situation in which he felt most comfortable, where he could explore Western harmony in the broad sense of the orchestra. Hearing music at a lot of different levels, Miles was constantly changing the personnel of his bands, with the exception of Chambers. Of his two recordings released in 1957, his lowest output since 1945, the first was a total success because it was planned and carried out with conviction, while the second, a film score, was a failure because he really didn't understand the film or the musical situation; in fact, the film seemed out of synchronization with the music. And, outside of Kenny Clarke, it wasn't Miles's band to begin with. The tenor player, Barney Wilen, had a very weak tone which Miles simply endured. There was nothing in the film score which bore any resemblance to anything Miles had played before or has since.

Julian "Cannonball" Adderley had come to New York with much fanfare and was even touted by some as the new Bird. Miles liked his sound and began playing gigs with him around New York. Miles always liked alto players with light and fast ones, in Parker's style, so Cannonball met the criteria; Miles even made the unusual gesture of doing a recording session with him under Adderley's name. Even though he himself had done a date with Michel Legrande earlier in 1958, it had been purely out of friendship, and Miles's name never appeared on the cover. So Miles showed he really wanted Cannonball in his band, and, when Trane reappeared, it became the finest band around. These three horn players were together for about a year and, during this time, Miles made the rare offer of putting them on a yearly salary. But in Cannonball and Trane there was too much leadership for such an arrangement, so salary arrangements never materialized.

The first rhythm section in Miles's sextet was Chambers, Philly Joe, and Garland, but a young, conservatory-trained pianist, Bill Evans, soon replaced Garland. Evans had been playing solo in between sets at the Village Vanguard, the Greenwich Village downstairs bar which was one of the few places Miles actually liked playing. Miles was intrigued by Evans' lyrical style and saw the possibilities of using him in his band to match his own lyricism juxtaposed to the blistering horns. Garland left, soon followed by Philly Joe, so Miles hired Jimmy Cobb, a percussionist of great skill but without the force and dynamism of Jones. The band was still a hard-playing one, but a lyrical, rhapsodic feeling sometimes predominated. It might even be said that this band was more concerned about lyricism on records than in its public appearances. "Green Dolphin Street," "Fran-Dance (Put Your Little Foot Out)," and later "So What" and "Blue in Green" are recorded testimony of Miles's intense lyricism. But the live band, whether at the Newport Jazz Festival or the Midway Lounge in Pittsburgh, burst with music. Solid, aggressive timbre marked this outfit, which almost mesmerized its audiences. With Evans, the band had five very distinctive solo voices: Miles, with his lines constantly changing through rhythmic phrases; Trane, exploring his instrument and harmony with scalar runs; Cannonball, becoming more mature and aggressive and growing just by standing beside Coltrane; Evans, a melodic player, rarely soloing on uptempo pieces; and Chambers, with his articulations now crystal clear. The band missed Garland's pinpoint accompaniment and his concept of piano playing.

It is always interesting to speculate on why people change the personnel in their bands, since it is usually a combination of many different reasons; sometimes a sideman may want to leave just to play his own music, or there may be a personality clash, or the leader may be looking for another kind of voice on a particular instrument. So it doesn't seem inconceivable that Miles, after recording again with Michel Legrande in mid-1958 and being impressed with the Frenchman's arrangements, heard Evans' voicings and decided to make a change in the piano style of his band.

After the above sextet literally zipped through the 1958 Newport Jazz Festival, playing five pieces in a little over half an hour, Miles made another orchestra date, to collaborate again with Gil Evans. In less than five months Miles had put together a band which was unquestionably the best he ever had and certainly one of the better bands in the history of African-American music. But his partnership with Gil Evans moved him into the orchestra of his mind, and together they produced a stunning version of *Porgy and Bess*. This effort, not as some say, *Sketches of Spain,* was the culmination of their achievement; *Spain* was popular because Miles had finally gone European, plus it picked up a few more customers by being *Down Beat's* Jazz Album of the Year, becoming a hip album to own. *Porgy and Bess,* using almost the same instrumentation as *Miles Ahead* (less one flute and one trumpet), combines two poetic spirits in a performance which is almost perfectly executed. As Billy Strayhorn was to Duke Ellington, Gil Evans' arrangements are tailor-made for Miles. And, as in *Miles Ahead,* it is Evans' unique accompanying arrangements that stand out. On "Summertime" he supports Miles with a seven-note motif which moves whole steps to the minor third, then skips to a major third; this juxtaposition of major and minor keys, a primary element of African-American music, further marks the composition in its opening with a descending major third (the accompaniment is ascending). Evans uses his knowledge of the music of Ellington and his great interest in the more traditional African-American forms to bring the two together, worked into closed position and harmonic movement in rhythms, providing the tuba and bass unison at the end of "The Buzzard Song," recorded at the third session on August 4. The usurpation of the tuba's reign by the acoustic bass culminated in the forties, so it is unique of Evans to combine the two instruments; but he always used tuba in his writing for Miles, with parts that speak to the skill of Bill Barber, who held that chair in all of the Davis/Evans ventures. Barber was not what one would call a jazz player, but his musicianship on the cumbersome tuba made him invaluable in this situation. The parts called for very well-controlled tone, dexterity of the fingers for the runs and leaps, and a keen sense of rhythm for the continual accent changes. In combination with Chambers, their execution was flawless. Musicianship was remarkably widespread by the late fifties, with more and more African-American musicians becoming literate. Paul Chambers was the personification of this, always ready to play.

On *Porgy and Bess,* each of the arrangements could be dissected, and the oneness that would appear between the two minds would be increasingly astonishing. Much of Miles's personality is introspective, almost withdrawn; this pensiveness manifests itself in these large orchestra works in streams of colors supplied by Gil Evans. Miles is most himself when telling a story: "Bess, You Is My Woman Now," "It Ain't Necessarily So," "I Love You, Porgy," "Bess, Oh Where Is My Bess," and "There's a Boat That's Leaving Soon for New York," all tales told this time by Miles Davis. The fact that he first played with Charlie Parker, undoubtedly learning to exploit the harmonic structure of any piece, makes his renditions of these pieces highly personal. Miles works closely with Evans, supplying rhythmic ideas and interpretations of the colors he wants from the orchestra. This is one of the few African-American/ European combinations that have worked, probably because it is neither artificial nor dreamed up by an advertising man, but a collection of ideas that took a long time to work out, discuss, and experiment with. Miles is the only soloist on *Porgy and Bess,* using both trumpet and flügelhorn. Yet, built in the arrangements, there are always lines for the different sections to weave around Miles, the nucleus of the effort.

The sextet was well known, if for no other reason, for keeping Miles from appearing at gigs which didn't provide a money guarantee. However, the band was popular even more because of its combined talents, exhibiting more gusto in personal appearances than on records. The fifth Newport Jazz Festival, in 1958, demonstrated the precision quality of the band, with the pieces played at faster tempos than those recorded in the studio. Although Miles was driving the group, making it play at its fullest potential, it appeared to the public, and especially to the so-called jazz critics, that he was being arrogant and almost indifferent. Nothing could be further from the truth. He had two horn players who were among the most gifted of their time, along with a dangerous rhythm section. Trane was constantly driving up against the barriers and bursting into the infinity of music. And he obviously found playing in the band a broadening experience:

> On returning, this time to stay until I formed my own group a few months ago, I found Miles in the midst of another stage of his musical de-

velopment. There was one time in his past that he
devoted to multichorded structures. He was interested in chords for their own sake. But now it
seemed that he was moving in the opposite direction to the use of fewer and fewer chord changes
in songs. He used tunes with free-flowing lines
and chordal direction. This approach allowed the
soloist the choice of playing chordally (vertically)
or melodically (horizontally).

In fact, due to the direct and free-flowing
lines in his music, I found it easy to apply the
harmonic ideas that I had. I could stack up chords
—say, on a C^7, I sometimes superimposed an E^{b7},
up to an $F^{\#7}$, down to an F. That way I could
play three chords on one. But on the other hand,
if I wanted to, I could play melodically. Miles's
music gave me plenty of freedom. It's a beautiful
approach.[18]

While the multichord structures, which were sometimes structures for their own sakes, stayed with the
large orchestra, the sextet moved on more in the direction of the modes and freer harmonic structures. The
music still had a center, but it acted as a tonic mode
through which a player could spin or plunge rather
than having constantly to move in harmonic maneuvers.
They provided what Coltrane, more than anyone else
in the band, needed most, some space to practice his
art. Under the influence of Miles and Trane, Adderley
used the band as a learning vehicle and played at least
as well as he has ever played. Although his tenure in
the band was short, Bill Evans had a profound effect
on Miles, moving him into the freer forms but with
much lyricism, so the music took on a somewhat breathy

[18] John Coltrane, "Coltrane on Coltrane," *Down Beat,* September
29, 1960, p. 31.

sound. He used long lines, sometimes without the peak and valley changes that the sextet itself always maintained.

After *Porgy and Bess*, the band played all around the country, and the music was deep. On March 2, 1959, Miles recorded his first pieces using modes. Bill Evans had already left the band, but Miles hired him to play on three of the five pieces recorded on two separate dates. The pieces "Flamenco Sketches," "All Blues," "So What," "Blue in Green," and "Freddie Freeloader" were a commercial success and helped liberate the music by developing less-structured forms, but they lacked any emotional drive; they just floated along like streamers in a ticker-tape parade. Much of the playing seemed too cautious, due to the fact that only Miles and Evans were familiar with the written music before the recording dates. The second session, on April 22, seemed more relaxed, but the music still was sluggish and low in its energy output. Here Miles was breaking out of old territory but being careful on the new ground. It seems that he underestimated the potential of the sextet by choosing to keep them in the dark about the music until he saw fit to enlighten them. On one hand, he demonstrated his confidence that the sextet could handle any situation by springing the music on them, but on the other hand, if the entire group could have shared in the development of these new ideas, then they could have gone much further ahead. However, Miles never really explored more deeply the possibilities of using modes, although, over a few years, he used them periodically.

The year 1959 saw a significant movement in the music of African-American people. At the end of February, Thelonious Monk took an eight-piece band into

Town Hall in New York and, playing only his own compositions, capped the hard bop era. The arrangements for this band were put together by a Juilliard instructor, the late Hall Overton, and they were exactly what Monk wanted. The long line written for the band at the end of "Little Rootie Tootie" is a composite of Monk's better-known piano phrases ingeniously strung together by Overton. This well-planned collaboration, along with the outstanding playing of trumpeter Donald Byrd, tenor saxophonist Charlie Rouse, alto saxophonist Phil Wood, baritone saxophonist Pepper Adams, the rhythm of Sam Jones, bass, and Art Taylor, percussion, enhanced Monk's style. He finally had the opportunity to exploit himself, and he took full advantage of it. The band had obviously made good use of its several rehearsal sessions. Donald Byrd, who was never known for his steady practice habits, was nonetheless particularly eloquent; especially adroit with Monk's changes, he dialogued with the music all night. But it was Monk's music, and it was he who provided the most sparkling playing with all its idiosyncrasies. He seemed to bounce off Jones and Taylor, and they, in turn, drove and generally added impetus to the whole proceedings. Thelonious Monk, the man who had been revered by his contemporaries but was unable to play in New York until 1957, finally cashed in.

In late autumn the Ornette Coleman Quartet arrived in New York. Coleman had spent a short time there in 1957 while he was studying at the School of Jazz at Music Inn, Lenox, Massachusetts. But this time, his moment, his appearance at the Five Spot brought the best kind of publicity, controversial. Everyone who heard the group was definite about what he heard, but different people heard a lot of different things.

Even Leonard Bernstein got into the act by supporting
Coleman, just the type of publicity Ornette needed. To
add more glamour to the situation, he was playing a
plastic saxophone, and it just so happened the last person who was recalled to have played a plastic alto was
Charlie Parker, when he first became known. Some
critics compared Coleman to Parker, saying that he
was the natural product because of his revolutionary
approach to music. His timbre was more human-sound-
ing, far from the pure sound of European saxophone
players, and his rhythm was much more consistently
free than had been heard before. More than anyone
else since Parker, Ornette kicked the music, expanded
its scope, provided new areas to explore with more emphasis on rhythm than European harmonically-moving
structures, whether they were major or minor scales or
modes. In bassist Charlie Haden and percussionist Edward Blackwell, he employed not only two most cred-
ible rhythm players but also students of the music who
continued to grow, to develop and make the music
move. The other member of the quartet, Don Cherry,
brought a new voice to cornet playing, although some
felt he stuttered and sputtered too much. But his lines
were inventive, and his rhythmic patterns connected
creatively. Occasionally Jimmy Garrison, the young
Philadelphia bassist, played, and sometimes Bill Hig-
gins would sit in on drums, so Coleman always had
well-equipped foundation people to go along with his
non-tonal lines. Much of the music Coleman played
reminded folks of bebop with its antilyrical changes;
the music bounced from register to register without
warning, adding freshness to it. Even the solitude of
"Lonely Woman," one of Ornette's first well-known
compositions, had wide interval jumps, not at all con-

ducive to voice. Usually in tunes like "Peace" there were subtle rhythm changes, the kind that most singers try to avoid, but still there was a haunting quality about both of these pieces that made them "catchy" to the listener. For a long time no band had risked significant changes in the music the way this one did. Becoming popular in the same year as Monk's landmark Town Hall concert only added to the impact it had on the people; when Monk's music was finally recognized, after his being ostracized fifteen years earlier, the people were also faced with the complexities of Ornette Coleman's music.

John Coltrane had made a dent by 1959 and his recordings, mostly sessions led by himself, without Miles, showed steady progress, while the lengths of some of his improvisations were setting new standards. This progress was not an attempt at catching up with anyone, because even this early, he was among the best tenor saxophonists; it's just that his playing showed steady development. He was improving his skills, always playing something new on his horn, just "chewing up" the harmonic system and unceasingly reaching out. He was a musician's musician and a man who was beginning to set a new style in his conduct in personal life. Cecil Taylor gets some small acknowledgments of his wonderful technique on piano, but only a few listeners saw the possibilities in music the way he did and still does. In the early sixties, Taylor employed such vanguard musicians as Jimmy Lyons, Archie Shepp, and Sonny Murray and, although recognized in only a limited circle, brought new percussive and linear innovations to the music. At times Taylor's playing was so vigorous and on-going that the percussionist rested in the middle of his long improvisations. At this time, too, Eric Dolphy played alto sax and bass clarinet right around the corner in the Chico Hamilton Quintet; it was his forthright playing in that band which gave Hamilton more exposure outside of Los Angeles. (Incidentally, Miles first met Hamilton when he was in Los Angeles in the late forties and it was his influence that got Hamilton a contract with Columbia in the sixties.)

At the other end of the spectrum, and probably more ominous, was the retirement of Sonny Rollins. With the affirmation of Trane, it was immediately assumed that Rollins had retired under fire, but that's because the public was stuck in the *Down Beat* syndrome of popularity and superiority. That Coltrane and Rollins were two very different players was obvious from the first time Trane played in the Miles Davis band, so to consider them competitively would require using criteria of proficiency invented by taste-makers who, more often than not, have no concept of the depth of the music; their style of comparative musicological study assumes that a "best" already exists. Rollins, highly influenced by Lester Young, played long lines of well-thought out, melodic songs, mostly slightly behind the beat. Trane was excavating, bellowing the horn to do more than it had ever done, with a hypnotic quality that confounded his critics. Primarily, Rollins retired because he found himself in bad health and recognized that it would never help his music; only a few have had the sense to understand that whatever damages physical and mental health is also bad for the music. Rollins is to be admired because, at a zenith in his career, he had the strength and insight to make a positive decision about himself. Not only did he work to regain his health, but he used the time to examine his own playing and find the kind of music he wanted to play, so he would never be forced into a situation where he would feel uncomfortable. When he first entered this voluntary confinement, many musicians tried to visit him, but he remained inaccessible, so great was his determination to be isolated. And with all this tremendous activity in African-American music, Miles, for the first time, was not in the vanguard.

By late spring in 1959, Cannonball had left the band, and Miles had returned to the quintet-size group. Pianist Wynton Kelly, who had been in the group for some time before Adderley left to form his own band, was the perfect combination of his predecessors, Garland and Evans; he used the subtle lyricism of Evans with the aggressive accompaniment of Garland. The quintet, now including Trane, Kelly, Chambers and Cobb, made an educational television show in which Miles was even able to bring in his orchestra, under the direction of Gil Evans. The quintet played "So What," a thirty-two-bar blues built on modes; it begins in Dorian for sixteen bars, moves a half-step to Hypolydian for eight, then back to Dorian for eight more. The orchestra backed up two years and played three pieces from the *Miles Ahead* sessions, showing they were trying to take advantage of the opportunity without being totally prepared for it and had to come up with something safe. Because the orchestra was included, this occasion demonstrates the great interest Miles had in the larger band; when the moment came to do TV, he wanted to make his mark a total success. However, just think of the impact he could have had if the orchestra had played some of the completely new music of which Miles has always been capable.

Miles had traveled to California earlier in the year and there he first heard Joaquin Rodrigo's "Concierto

De Aranjuez for Guitar and Orchestra." The music impressed him so much that when he next saw Gil Evans, he had him listen to it, and they subsequently turned out *Sketches of Spain.* The album was immeditely a popular success, but, in actuality, it was lacking the basic ingredient of African-American music, rhythm; the music itself is stunning vertically, but it has very little interest horizontally. Nowhere does it have the spiritual power of *Porgy and Bess.* The tempos are purposely kept very slow and many times are free; that is, the music is often moving without pulse, and when there is a pulse, it sounds artificial, like third stream music. The album drew on the main trick bag of African-American music, in which it is assumed that the music improves by the application of European classical techniques. In reality, these techniques have shackled the music, kept it bottled in tonal centers. But the third stream music was cresting on popularity and Gunther Schuller was a longtime friend of Miles. Parker also had an interest in European classical music; just before he died, he was working with composer Edgard Varèse on some musical projects. Two of his closest musical friends, Michel Legrande and André Hodeir, were in the French avant-garde musical scene although they both have strong commitments to African-American music. Miles may have been obsessive about European classical music, but only a few of his contemporaries weren't, and I would hasten to bet that many of today's players carry the same burden. Isn't that what Ornette Coleman's "Skies of America" is about?

Sketches of Spain is a beautiful artistic endeavor. It took two dates to complete, with basically the same orchestra as the two previous large group sessions. Miles is playing slowly, methodically, and, for the first time, using extensively bent notes. Also for the first time, the orchestration, with its colors streaming like a series of rainbows, definitely telling a story, seems to be what Miles primarily wants. Although he and the orchestra are almost antiphonal, it is a true dialogue, as between a preacher and his congregation. A harp is added, Trane plays tenor, and there is no alto saxophone; there are two percussionists, Jimmy Cobb and Elvin Jones, with the latter playing castanets and other assorted Spanish percussive instruments. The Rodrigo concerto is played as a framework for Miles's improvisations to muse around. The orchestra parts dominate even though they bear little resemblance to the original work, with Miles playing spurts here and there. Without question, the aim was to get an overall sound and not to highlight the soloist. On "The Pan Piper," "Solea," "Will o' the Wisp," and "Saeta" Miles plays as creatively in that penetrating style as he ever played. The mood created by the music is melancholy, but one of the captivating features of Miles's music is his use of dissonances. Miles uses quarter tones as well as anyone who has every played this music, and nowhere does he use them as effectively as on *Sketches of Spain.*

The second session of *Sketches* was on March 11, 1960, and immediately afterward Miles was on his way to London. His English trip was an artistic success, but the critics found his abrasive style not too reverent; his habit of leaving the stage when the other players were soloing didn't seem quite right, and his hoarse voice eliminated long-winded, repetitive interviews which would have been on non-musicological subjects anyway. He went to Sweden on a concert tour which somehow ended with Trane leaving the band. The effect of his departure on Miles was really staggering, and the succession of sidemen that followed demonstrated Miles's extended grappling with the situation. He had been a New York musician for fifteen years and a most pioneering one. For most of the last five years John Coltrane had been his partner, and Miles had watched him grow, night after night, from a stumbling but vigorous tenor player whom he overshadowed to a powerful force who challenged and drove him to all the established boundaries of music; Coltrane's leaving was inevitable, but Miles's reaction to it was probably not what he had expected of himself. The fact was that he now had the awesome responsibility of replacing John Coltrane, the most revolutionary player of his time. Impossible!

Miles's first choice as replacement was an alto player, Sonny Stitt. It was an interesting selection, because Sonny had always been mentioned as the sure successor to Charlie Parker and, though he had a remarkable technique on both alto and tenor, he never quite had that spark that any successor would need. Stitt made a return trip to Sweden with Miles late in the year, but was soon replaced by tenor man Hank Mobley. Mobley had been associated with Art Blakey's mid-fifties Jazz Messengers band which included trumpeter Kenny Dorham, Doug Watkins on bass and pianist Horace Silver. The exact opposite of Trane, Hank was a slow, almost lazy player with very little emotion in his music. Kelly and Miles now provided the strong voices in the band, with Miles playing more mute than ever and doing it particularly well. But a musician like Mobley slows the music down, while Miles and Trane used to set a blistering pace. When Miles had Trane and Cannonball in the band he could play for as long or as short as he wanted to, knowing that they would hold up their own ends. Now he had to carry the band, but it seemed as if this just lifted him to a stronger position, for his playing was more consistent than ever. He was really into his instrument technically and was influencing every young trumpeter coming along.

Demonstrating how difficult it is to maintain a high level of music, Miles now began his second transitional period, in which his musical movements seemed to contradict his established style. But technically his playing was still together, so it must have been what and with whom he was playing that threw it out of synchronization. For two years Miles continued in this stage, the likes of which all musicians must face (and only those totally concentrating on music ever bridge), as they attempt to reestablish their music in their own minds. As he played a conglomeration of his "hits" with a horn sideman whose style and approach were totally different from his, and finally changing his entire rhythm section (which had still included Paul Chambers), Miles's music faltered. After the success of *Sketches of Spain,* he decided to exploit the orchestra further by combining it with his quintet in a concert at Carnegie Hall, New York City, on May 19, 1961. Although the quintet played well enough on "So What," the music was obviously out of kilter; the orchestra was not as honed as it had been on its recordings, leading one to believe that there might have been a lot of technology, fitting parts and/or sections together; if this is true, then bringing an unprepared orchestra to this most significant concert was a mistake. Miles hadn't been back too long from a series of California concerts with the quintet, and, given his usual methodical style of doing things, he was short on time for putting this concert together.

After this, Miles began to work with different-sized bands, sometimes a quintet and occasionally, a sextet, with a trombone added. He used J. J. Johnson for a short time and then Frank Rehak, who had been in the large orchestra. But the trombone wasn't to his liking so he started to concentrate on the quintet, which was now manned by younger musicians, musicians, someone once noted, who grew up on *his* music. He had recorded with tenor saxophonist Wayne Shorter on what now looks like something he would rather forget, a very sad session which included a singer named Bob Dorough. The entire product was unfortunate except for Shorter, who blew lustily with Blakey's Messengers. Miles wanted to hire him on the spot, but Shorter was unsure about getting his own compositions played in Miles's band and also had a strong commitment to Blakey. So, early in 1963, Miles hired George Coleman who, for many years, had been the bellwether of the "Slide" Hampton bands. Coleman, a very strong player with knowledge of the rudiments of the music, read the band's music very well. More than anything else, his playing complemented Miles's with good hard bop, changing tempo lines. But most significant for Miles was the personnel change at bass; for the first time in seven years, except for various out periods, Chambers was not in the band. He left to join his buddies Wynton Kelly and Jimmy Cobb, and they toured for some time after that as the Wynton Kelly Trio; Kelly was deaf in one ear but had perfect pitch in the other, playing outstanding piano. He was also a good bassist and an excellent tenor saxophonist.

Ron Carter was Miles's new bassist. After two years things were beginning to take a permanent shape again, and the choice of Carter reflected Miles's astute selection processes. With strong musicianship, conservatory-trained (Eastman School of Music) Carter had outstanding skills on both the double bass and the cello and was extremely versatile; he had been associated with the younger new music players and was clearly first-class. His flexibility kept him moving, so he was in and out of the band except at recordings, in which he was used almost exclusively over the next five years. The second key member in the quintet was Tony Williams, the very gifted seventeen-year-old percussionist whom Miles first saw in the Jackie McLean band. Williams had grown up in Boston and had been tutored by Alan Dawson, the great Boston percussionist, and Sam Rivers, multi-instrumentalist and composer. He had played in Rivers' experimental band in concerts with the Boston Improvisational Ensemble, so he was ready when he stepped into Miles's band to become the strongest of Miles's drummers since Philly Joe Jones. The last rhythm player to enter this phase of Miles's music was Herbie Hancock, on piano. Hancock had also studied at a conservatory (Roosevelt University, Chicago) and was a very skilled musician when he joined the band, especially in using long lines and in employing the left hand to accompany the right. On top of his solo skills, Hancock was superb in his accompaniment, not only playing stimulating progressions but redirecting and reshaping rhythms and tempos. This new rhythm section was young, schooled and relatively experienced—the most flexible yet. To avoid a senseless comparison of individuals, suffice it to say that this team made the people play. And, in spite of whatever anyone felt about Miles's stage presence, the band popped.

As was his custom, Miles took this new band into the studio and recorded enough music to complete a date started in Los Angeles. Having recorded live only three times in his seventeen professional years, the first time in 1958, Miles now recorded three successive live dates in a little over a year. The first was on July 27, 1963, at the annual Jazz Festival at Antibes, France. Even though they had been together for only a few months, the band was very intimate in the flawless way it grasped the music which Miles had been playing for years. On this date, it sounded fresh, although it still overemphasized harmonic schemes; the only new piece was "Joshua" by Victor Feldman, an English pianist with whom Miles had played briefly while on the West Coast. The group fired one piece after another, mostly in up-tempos, and quickly exited. Their musicianship was on the highest level throughout this performance, and the rhythm, in the tradition of the music of the people, sparkled. George Coleman played well, but for some reason his music wasn't developing at the expected rate. He still complemented Miles with consistent, harmonically modulating lines. Hancock blossomed, and his accompaniment gave Miles plenty of space to deal with his short rhythmic phrases. His soloing was technically impeccable, always on top of the beat, changing the tempos, then the rhythms. Even at this early stage, he was unquestionably the finest all-around pianist Miles had ever had in any of his bands. Williams was truly one of the most skilled young percussionists ever to come along, and his poise and knowledge of rhythms reflected his early training and his teachers. He was one of two highly skilled percussionists in Boston at this time; in fact, some thought that Miles originally wanted to hire the other, Clifford Jarvis, but decided on Williams instead.

Once again, Miles had to decide when to have a recording session, an event which all musicians must deal with although, most of the time, their hands are tied because of contractual arrangements. Miles had agreed to do a benefit for CORE (Congress of Racial Equality) in the beginning of 1964, so he had it recorded—perhaps unwisely, because most of the music was what Miles had been playing for years. This concert was held at New York's Philharmonic Hall, which had just recently opened, and the audience's response was gratifying, to say the least. The total energy level between the performers and the spectators set sparks flying; this was the effect that Miles could have on an audience with the penetrating, masterful way he played "Stella by Starlight" or "My Funny Valentine." The band played twelve pieces, an unusually high number for Miles at a single concert. Ideally, a man should record when he has something different happening, not just when he is playing outstanding music in a well-known form; but, by the beginning of 1964, music had become a financial as well as an artistic endeavor to Miles. His relationship to the other band members became more a business association rather than the close, binding friendships he used to have in the earlier groups. He infrequently rehearsed with the band as a whole, expecting the older members to stay in touch with the newer members in terms of the music. In 1964 he changed his horn sideman twice. The first replacement, Sam Rivers, a very creative but relatively unknown tenor saxophonist, learned most of Miles's repertoire by practicing with Hancock and Williams. He had been hired for Miles's first trip to Japan, the country that had become a hotbed for African-American music, and he and Miles talked about the music only just before their first concert. Rivers was the strongest horn player for Miles's band since Trane and showed more potential, since it was already so realized, than any of his successors in the band. Yet Miles let him go after a little over six months. They were in Japan for a month and did a series of concerts which produced one album, never released in the United States; they also did a number of concerts across the States. Rivers' playing, as evinced by the tape from Japan, was searching and powerful, not tied into traditional centers but more into rhythms.

Wayne Shorter had been Miles's choice for over two years, and when he was finally available, he jumped at the chance to complete the quintet again. On the third live date in September of '64 in Berlin, Wayne was present, and, although the material they played then was Miles's old stuff, the cooperation would bear fruit in the beginning of 1965 on *E.S.P.* But 1964 was an extraneous year of hassles for Miles Davis, a year in which his public criticism of Eric Dolphy in a most negative manner was published only sixteen days before Dolphy died. It was also known that Miles had been trying to get Dolphy to join his band, the same year that Dolphy was making headlines in Europe playing in Trane's band and only three years after Dolphy had orchestrated Trane's brilliant *Africa* album.

E.S.P., a collection of compositions contributed by the band members with the exception of Williams, was a decided departure from Miles's usual style. The music became more rhythmic, especially moving to more juxtaposed rhythms, but still very centered. The music of India, perhaps the most extensively improvised music in the world, most often has a drone which accompanies in tonic and dominant; it is apparent that Miles, at least here, advances complex rhythms while continuing harmonic or center changes. Adding the tempo variations and the musicianship of the band, the music sounds excellent. The piece "Agitation," written by Miles, moves with precision. Ron Carter, particularly strong, moves in and out of tempo and rhythm changes like a gazelle leaping through the savannahs of Africa. However, he then put himself into a repetitious pattern on his own composition "Mood," one of the contradictions which faulted this particular band of Miles's. This was Miles's flawless quintet crescendoing and decrescendoing in sixteen-bar sequences. The quintet seemed like air going in and then out of a balloon, increasing the intensity up to a certain point, then letting the piece resolve slowly. Execution was the hallmark of this band, in which Miles responded more to Herbie Hancock and was more influenced by him than any of his other pianists, which is remarkable, especially considering that, for the major part of his career, Miles had related more to the bass and percussion. Miles's music became more beautiful than revolutionary.

It now becomes a question of what the music called "jazz" is all about. In 1964, Miles had attempted to underpay Eric Dolphy by chastising him in the media. Considering the type of musicians Miles always selected for his bands, it seems unlikely he underestimated Dolphy's musicianship. In that same year he fired Sam Rivers, who was then acknowledged by his peers as one of the stronger tenor saxophonists playing the music. If so-called jazz is the revolutionary idiom of African-

American music, then it can be said that Miles was settling into hard bop as his motif for expression. All around him the music was moving toward more free and changing mechanisms, especially concerning liberation from harmonic structure and more connection with multidirectional rhythms. Miles clearly saw the implication of combining rhythms but, like so many hard bop players, felt the need to give his audiences harmonic relationships; one could recognize a movement in the music, could anticipate what was going to happen. He became a traditional player, in spite of the fact that he was playing the most innovative music in that tradition. The choice of Shorter offers an even better perspective of where Miles, at least at this time, was most comfortable. Here was an excellent tenor saxophonist whose skills and techniques collaborated in long melodic lines but whose leanings toward the rhapsodic had mellowed out his strength. One of the intangibles of this music is emotional toughness, the ability to cope with all of the diverse elements of one's music. By the time Wayne began to play with Miles, his tone had become round rather than hard and his articulation muttered by the use of too many sliding phrases. Miles's power just enveloped both him and his musical personality. Given the choice between two very venturesome players and a competent sideman, Miles chose the latter. This has been true of his selections since John Coltrane left the band.

Trane's career was soaring at an unbelievable rate with uncompromising progress in his music. Never patient with inertia, much less stagnation, he became identified with the younger, new music musicians, joining forces with Dolphy, Archie Shepp, and most of the fresh (as distinguished from stale) players. He had also begun his long trip into the musical thought of Eastern music; those investigations were beginning to manifest their effects as early as 1961, and, by 1964, he had become the guru for most younger musicians. His quartet of bassist Jimmy Garrison, pianist McCoy Tyner, and percussionist Elvin Jones made a historic imprint on the music. Their music was very liberated, with the length and intensity of the collective improvisations setting new standards for public performances. Trane was the master in the forging of the new music, bringing credence to it with his incredible musicianship. Miles was now the master in the era which ended a tradition, a long, hard struggle through European music theories with European instruments; he is a very individualistic player, with a mind that can add long columns of numerals almost instantly. Never relying on extended solos, his whole shaping experience originated in hearing harmonic changes in the music. Even the rhythmic forms, first getting more frenzied and then calm, seemed fixed from one piece to another, especially on *E.S.P.*

Miles and Trane were in contact, often exchanging information about available talent for last-minute gig replacements. Reggie Workman, a bassist who had worked with Trane off and on in the early sixties, occasionally replaced Carter. Miles was working rather consistently now, traveling not only throughout the United States but also around the world, so he needed to know who was in New York with good skill and ready to go at a moment's notice. Trane was certainly someone whose advice Miles sought on such matters, but when it came to the gigs he wanted to be really stellar, he would use his quintet; on these occasions, the band played Miles's older material, mostly in very up-tempos with just a short hint of written material. Much of the harmonic material was opening up, and the band became closer and tighter in its total musicianship. If the audiences could anticipate the music through progressions, then the possibilities of this gifted band were almost infinite, although it was still using a redundant system. Yet it was well over a year and a half before Miles went into the studio after the *E.S.P.* collection. Perhaps it was due to the rigorousness of career and the traveling, although he had been doing it for quite some time. He was still playing the same music in his public appearances which he began playing some fifteen years earlier and, even though to his audiences it was a welcome relief from the new music players, it showed no real development or movement on his part. Keep in mind that the quintet included Shorter, Carter, Hancock and Williams, who played together for four years (1964 to 1968).

Then in October of 1966, they made a record date, in two sessions, containing all new music except for an absolutely brilliant performance of Eddie Harris' "Freedom Jazz Suite." The material was new in its melodic content with more freedom in its movement; it seemed that in his slow, methodical way of doing things, Miles was moving the band into more open pastures, although the pieces were still tight in their execution. This date was followed by six others in the middle of May, 1967, which further indicated an opening up of his music. These combined sessions contributed fourteen new pieces, with the music more free than it had ever been, the strongest since Coltrane had left the band. Most of the pieces were short lines from which to jump off, like "Madness" or "Riot." The band seemed quite at home, with the exception of Shorter, whose energy was very low and who stayed close to the lines on many of the tunes during his improvisations. But there was also "Nefertiti," a piece which states the line over and over while Williams plays solo, and the repetitive "Fall," a melancholy piece. So even in the very fresh music of this period, Miles inserted compositions which had a very conservative flavor to them, "peeping" but not quite totally committed.

When John Coltrane died on July 17, 1967, it seemed that more and more of the responsibility for leading the music would fall on Miles. Unlike most of his contemporaries, he had continued to grow, although his progress was somewhat slow. Over the last few years his music had become more free, and occasionally his band would play new material in their public performances; but, like any famous artist, he felt some responsibility to return to some of his older, more well-known pieces in his repertoire. It had been over three years since he had recorded any of his public appearances, except those still in the Columbia can. In the beginning of 1968 he recorded one piece, "Paraphernalia," using guitarist George Benson; this was the first time he had ever used this instrument, and it could have indicated a new direction in which he was heading. But soon he was back with Gil Evans again, although the Evans things were not very successful this time. Miles, somewhat influenced by Hancock, then decided to add the electric piano to the group, which immediately had two results: the first, recorded on May 15 through 17, produced "Country Son," "Black Comedy," and "Stuff," and Hancock's work was stimulating, but the band was uncohesive, rushing the music. Because of its continuing use of electricity, this band, which had been together for four years, was not changing in personnel but in its notion of developing away from natural instrumentation. Miles, never known for long solos, concentrated on suites where the music would change tempo and rhythm to indicate a different part of the total effort. The second recording at the end of June was more significant because, on two pieces, there were key personnel changes: on "Petits Machins" and "Mademoiselle Mabry" bassist Dave Holland replaced Ron Carter, and pianist Chick Corea sat in Hancock's chair. This was the first time in five years that Miles had used substitutes for these two magnificent performers, and remarkably there was no discernible change in the music. Holland had gigged throughout Europe, and Miles had first seen him in his native country, England. Customarily, when he played somewhere, Miles would attempt to hear the other musicians performing in the area; doing this, he was immediately impressed with Holland's first-rate technique. When it became apparent that Carter would not be available on an ongoing basis, Miles phoned Holland and asked him to join the band. Tony Williams had first approached Chick Corea, and then Miles called him as well. Corea was surprised that the music was still very much centered, but he saw that more and more space was opening up. Corea's style is so close to Hancock's that, although Herbie had dominated the chair for four years, Corea fit in beautifully because of the similarity in their playing. They were both strong accompanying pianists. In fact, Chick originally thought that was why he was hired, but he found that, with the increased use of the electric piano, he was playing more linear things and even following lines in his accompaniment. So the transition from one player to the other was smooth.

The music of the collection known as *Filles de Kilimanjaro* includes the two pieces mentioned above plus "Frelon Brun," "Tout de Suite," and "Filles de Kilimanjaro," all written by Miles. These compositions had a strong tempo/rhythm impact, suggesting that Miles had made a decision to stay with combined rhythms going in multiple directions but in music that was either tonal or related to some kind of tonic. He moves in and out of the major and minor scales and modes, with much of the structure in the rhythm. Many of the pieces begin in distortions, and almost all go through involved arrangements, not tone poems, but different statements. The music was beginning to take on a rock feeling, with the energy level very controlled. Except in "Petits Machins," the improvisations all sound as though they have been written out.

The February 16, 1969, session of "In a Silent Way" is a continuation of this development, only with longer, better-organized improvisations. The pieces are related even though there are four parts. Miles uses three pianists, a guitarist, and Shorter on soprano, for the first time in a session. The biggest drawback of this whole scheme of music, dating from "Sorcerer" through this album, is the feeling that something is going to happen—but it never does. The music rarely bursts open, although Miles consistently plays well. It is all very mechanical, sometimes even contrived, but always expertly executed. It isn't really loose, and the players are doing nothing but playing beautiful music. Perhaps that's why Miles used John McLaughlin, the brilliant English guitarist, to further these streams of lines for their own sakes. Interestingly enough, he also used pianist Joe Zawinul in combination with Corea and Hancock, three musicians whose styles were very close, with each playing organ or electric piano. Although Miles kept moving away from natural instruments, employing more and more European techniques, the music still had some inventiveness to it. Miles's music always draws great interest even during its most challenging periods. However, at no time during his career was his public music so different from his recorded music. This increasingly widening gap was becoming a problem.

Miles was as concerned about his record sales with Columbia as they were. His last and only 100,000 sale was *Porgy and Bess,* over ten years earlier. Most of the other albums had sold around 50,000 copies, but the last two or three were having trouble hitting 25,000. It was more of a comment on the music, that it was changing too slowly and certainly wasn't keeping up with the followers of Trane. Columbia noticed the sales drop, and president Clive Davis advised Miles to change his music to accommodate a larger audience.[19] Mr. Clive Davis is an attorney, and attorneys usually become presidents of large record companies because they can read contracts. When an artist is in a position where, because the culture of his people is not recognized, he must make a decision whether he will allow himself to be exploited for the sake of record sales, he either has to move to another record company or produce by himself. Either choice has its own very definite hazards: Columbia had always treated Miles well, and besides, using another company would mean dealing with people who couldn't have the total resources of Columbia; self-producing would mean doing everything from soup to nuts. The kind of change his public wanted from Miles's band was more explosiveness. On

[19] Dan Morgenstern, "No Jive from Clive," *Down Beat,* September 16, 1971, p. 18.

the other hand, the kind of change that Columbia wanted was catering to young rock fans, which would take him out of the forefront of African-American music. No matter who you are or what your status in musical life is, if you are playing African-American music and you are African-American, you will ultimately be forced into making an important decision that will either strengthen your music or compromise it. Obvously Miles was upset that the company would have the audacity to ask him to change his music to accommodate anyone, because he had never compromised, not even to please his audiences. His first response was to ask for his release, but he reconsidered, and then he relented.

Money has a remarkable effect on this country and its people, though it is monopolized by people who know how to make profit. The culture of African-American people has been exploited for every drop of energy it has. What was happening to Miles Davis was a loss of income and some luxuries, which he wasn't ready for. It must have been discouraging to have to deal with a man who had no interest in the music for its own sake, and who had no interest in Miles Davis except financial exploitation. Until institutions are developed to serve only the music, its practitioners, and students, there will always be a Miles Davis, a person whose strength and uncompromising musical position encourages other struggling musicians trying to play the music of African-American people without sacrifice to the pressures of money. To expect the compromise not to happen is naïve, but when it does, especially to a person who has resisted as long as Miles had, it pulls the plug on one's fantasies.

When Miles called Clive Davis and told him he

was prepared to overhaul the music so it would have more broad-based appeal, the president of Columbia records promised Miles an extensive, well-coordinated national promotional campaign on this new music. The result was the 1970 spring release of *Bitches Brew* which, by the autumn of 1971, had sold over 400,000 copies in this country alone. Miles had given signs of what would be coming when he played both the Fillmore East and Fillmore West during 1970. He had made about thirty albums with Columbia, but the new album sold more than all of the previous releases. Including McLaughlin, Holland, Zawinul, Corea and Shorter, the list of players on *Bitches Brew* had increased and changed. Jack DeJohnette had replaced Tony Williams on percussion on a permanent basis, although Miles also used several other percussionists—Lenny White, Jim Riley, and Charles Alias—for this date. DeJohnette, though a superior traps player, was relegated to slapping the drums in the style of white rock music. It was this general placement of musicians into roles too cramped for their potential that made this new format so illogical. Miles Davis became a household word at the expense of his own creativity and the intrinsic value of his whole band.

The avant-garde wing of African-American music will probably never be popular. It has never been embraced by African-American people, because we have believed that whatever music we create can only benefit from the advice and influence of the dominant culture. It is this popularizing belief that finally conquered Miles. Employing more white players, though the level of musicianship may not have faltered, he was keeping money out of the hands of his brothers. It is really more a question of economics and loyalty than a racial issue.

Playing in Miles's band would give a boost to anyone's career, such is the nature of his prestige and importance among his contemporaries. Now he decided to give credence to musicians whose talents merited it, but the distinction could have been better and more constructively used by black musicians, who had to bear the pains of economic survival while striving to play the best music possible. There are many rationales for not hiring one's brothers, which have nothing to do with music. So Miles moved away from the mainstream of African-American music, playing the best rock around, using all the technical gimmicks he could put his hands on in order to create a super-music. He was putting his music into computers along with echo chambers, Wa-Wa pedals, electric pianos, and every other conceivable trick to expand and give credibility to a music that was artistically far beneath his potential.

The *Bitches Brew* collection was followed by a record of a live performance, the first live release since 1964. The music was the same as *Bitches Brew* except that a soprano sax player named Steve Grossman had replaced Wayne Shorter. Some of the music sounds as if it is coming straight from the synthesizer in a very European way. Missing also are Bennie Maupin, who played bass clarinet on *Brew,* and Harvey Brooks, who played Fender bass. The music was the same in spite of the changes; this was one of the few times in Miles's recent musical history that he played the same music in public as on his records. Perhaps the most significant addition was Airto Moriera, the Brazilian percussionist whose assortment of instruments was the only natural thing happening. *In Person* was followed by the film score *Jack Johnson, Live/Evil,* and *On the Corner,* each album maintaining very rhythmic rock music. After

Johnson, the young alto sax player Gary Bartz replaced Grossman, and Keith Jarrett played piano. Carlos Garnett later replaced Bartz as horn sideman. These really dangerous sidemen couldn't move the music from the rut in which it had settled. Bartz was the strongest horn sideman since Trane, particularly adept at developing long, rhythmic lines; his sound was more robust than most of his predecessors, and his ability with the blues was uncanny. Garnett is the only musician on *On the Corner* actually worth listening to. Miles plays so little that it is difficult to make an assessment. Keith Jarrett, who had been a sideman with tenor saxophonist Charles Lloyd for a long time, continued his nervous but creative work with Miles, but not even their strong musical personalities could overcome the force that was keeping the music on the treadmill of conformity.

The sixties decade was a slow diminishing period for Miles. It marked the end of his fruitful association with John Coltrane and his move toward using younger musicians in his band. It also marked the end of demanding horn sidemen to push Miles into unexplored areas of music. After Trane and Cannonball left the band, a real void resulted which has never been filled. Miles kept a strong rhythm section, but pianist Hancock wanted to play in center court, and the infusion of the electric piano in the late sixties drew the group into the controlled avant-garde European sound, moving it away from highly spontaneous music. The band's public appearances were once again decidedly different from its recorded documents, with the live band more aggressive in its approach to music. Miles was no longer the progressive leader of the music, and his protégé John Coltrane was playing the most revolutionary music of his time. During this period, he only occasionally experimented with the size of the band and rarely with the instrumentation. Even though he won most of the popular awards in the music industry, his record sales leveled off and then drastically declined. With the exception of Ron Carter, the members of his band were not fresher-playing musicians, and even those who have left the group are permanently tainted. With all this in the background, in the beginning of the seventies, Miles Davis was ripe for exploitation.

The most significant aspects of the seventies' musical activities of Miles Davis are his album covers and the names of new pieces. Of the five albums released, three covers show beauty juxtaposed to grossness. No one realizes what he has done to his music more than Miles himself. He titles pieces with his own names spelled backwards, perhaps indicating that life is one coin with two sides, that good and evil are coexistent. For twenty-eight years he has provided more consistently good music than any of his peers. The doubt about the music today does not come from the musicianship but from his choice of idiom. His recent appearances, especially with Bartz, DeJohnette, and Jarrett, and now with Carlos Garnett, all indicate the potential is still there, and often it is realized. His music is still very complex, not only in its structures but also in the multiple levels on which it communicates. The machines which fortify the band and the amount of time it takes to assemble and disassemble them somewhat detract from the musical impression. But the music bellows and dances out to the people even though it is no longer ritual but social music. Seeing Miles play has always been a pleasurable musical experience. Now the music is not as demanding to listen to as it once was, and the whole emphasis is extramusical, with clothes, machines, and even the mannerisms of the players pulling one's interest away from the music itself. Tallying all the pluses and minuses of Miles's musical career, it is clear that he is a musician of intrinsic intellect. He associated with two of the greatest musical minds this country has ever produced, Coltrane and Parker, and to think those relationships weren't musically reciprocal is a mistake. He has consistently written music and made significant contributions to all of the large orchestra sessions. His rhythm sections have always been superior in terms of technique, flexibility, and knowledge of rhythm, the essence of African-American music.

Laudably, Miles Davis has survived and remains intact. Trying to play artistic African-American music in this country is musical suicide. Given the nature of the life style, the competition, the constant bribes which tempt artists to conform to some uneducated concept of music, it is surprising that his music continued to grow and stay healthy. Add to this the humiliations that an African-American artist has to suffer living in a country that despises his people, and it becomes clear how hard it is not to compromise the music, just to take some pressure off his back. It is downright impossible to maintain a constant flow of exceptional music despite poor working conditions and the practically nonexistent respect for the music. For many years Miles Davis has carried more than his share of the responsibility for the development of African-American music. It is time for someone else to carry the load.

STYLE

Before going into any detailed discussion of the style of Miles Davis, I feel obliged to define just what I mean by style in this context. Of all the words that are synonymous with style, "idiosyncrasies" best fits my objective; that is, the things that Miles consistently does which make his playing a particular style in itself. Many of those things have been documented in the appendix: the transcriptions, the recording sessions, and even the bibliography. These are the literate aspects of Miles's music: the analysis, the categorizations of melody, rhythm, and harmony. But the music of African-American people has always been nonliterate. Until recently, its instrumentalists have mostly been nonliterate and their music improvised, created on the spot. It stands to reason that if Miles is to be understood, it must be in his total idiosyncratic form, not just by interpretation of his music but of his total musical mind, which literacy only begins to explain. So, in examining this man's music, I find it necessary from time to time to speculate on the particular quality of musicianship that applies to African-American music.

Miles Davis is a revolutionary musician. He came to the music with great potential but with limited skills on the instrument he chose to play, the trumpet. Historically the trumpet was a proud instrument, played powerfully in a staccato pattern. The masters of its higher register were always the acclaimed players. The trumpet was once king, and its early practitioners, Buddy Bolden and Joe Oliver, affirmed that monarchy. As the music itself changed, the trumpet's position in it changed as well, although it was a trumpeter, Louis Armstrong, who brought about the changes precipitating the ascent of the saxophone. Armstrong explored the melodic possibilities and demonstrated that the trumpet was more than a bludgeoning tool. Miles's first professional teacher, Dizzy Gillespie, had perfected the Armstrong tradition and, ironically, suggested to Miles that he inquire into his own head and investigate where he himself heard music. Miles did so and brought about a significant change in trumpet playing and in the music itself.

There are certain generalizations one can make about Miles's playing. Largely, he doesn't play long solos, so they are rarely frivolous. In standing next to John Coltrane and Charlie Parker, both embellishing players, his economy of music space fit naturally. During his harmonic period when he would play line after line of modulating scales, Trane, in admiration of Miles, sometimes castigated himself, admitting that his solos could be condensed but he didn't know how. After this period when Trane began to scrutinize rhythmic movement more, the length of his solos began to take on

more meaning. Miles's improvisations, logically following the brevity of his solos, are generally short rhythmic
statements which he sends out with great intensity. Although now capable in all registers, he is a middle
register player and exploits both the upper and lower
registers to accentuate what he is doing in the center.
The penetrating feeling he conveys in his music is the
result of his being one of those musicians, usually ex-
ceptionally gifted, who knows how to accent music in
the right places and at the right times. Miles can pull
his audiences into the music through the way he shapes
his solos rhythmically, where the accents fall, demonstrating his affinity for this music. He knows how to
blow into his instrument with a controlled air stream,
allowing him to burst a phrase or slowly crescendo and
decrescendo a note. Never a virtuoso in the traditional
mechanisms of playing a European instrument, he has
become a virtuoso in his style. He changed and expanded on the basic concepts of the instrument, daring
to be different and seek new avenues of expression.
He has influenced many trumpet players and exploded
the myth of the "right" way to play an instrument.

Miles's early professional years, from 1945 to 1948,
were rough. Not one to waste any opportunity, he used
those years to formulate and struggle with his own
ideas. More often than not, he spit in the horn when
he was playing and languished in the middle register.
Playing beside Parker so unnerved him occasionally
that one could hear the noise of saliva moving through
the tubes of his trumpet while he played his solos. He
was a patient, hard-working student who had taken
advantage of his time at Juilliard to learn all he could
about harmony and the piano. He had terrible trouble
with up-tempo pieces and, since this was bebop's forte,

he sometimes sounded as if he was sliding home from
third base throughout his improvisations. His embouchure wasn't strong and many times failed him, causing
his sound to waver. He had all the problems that a
novice would have playing beside a genius. He learned
much about music, and Parker, in turn, put Miles's
great talent to good use.

The sessions at Capitol bore the fruits of Miles's
labor. His tone wasn't really strong and he sometimes
rushed his solos, but he was comfortable in this setting.
The solos were short, many only one chorus. Most of
the pieces were in medium tempo so Miles could weave
and string short phrases together in that great symmetrical way for which he is so famous. His propensity
for centered music bears out this need for structure and
tight-fittedness. The music of these sessions was very
unemotional, not cold but professional. So it is evident
in one of the pieces, "Godchild," recorded on January
21, 1949, how well he organized his whole solo into a
complete statement by carefully balancing the phrases.[20]
The solo is only one chorus long (32 bars), and is a
combination of multiples of three. It begins at the
pickup with two three-note phrases, then on to a seven-
note phrase followed by a six-, eight-, and ending with
an eighteen-note phrase before the first double bar at
measure eight. The next eight measures begin with
two two-note phrases, then a six-note, four-note, and a
two-note phrase, followed by another six-note phrase,
ending with a ten-note phrase. This is followed by five
phrases, almost all equal, and closes with a straight
run of eight sixteenth notes. Then the last four unequal
phrases end in another eighteen-note phrase. There

[20] Lloyd Lifton's accurate transcription of this solo can be found
in *Down Beat*, July 10, 1969, p. 42.

definitely are four eight-bar statements, each complete in itself; one with four phrases, the next five with two broken statements, the following five somewhat symmetrical, and the last four disjunct phrases. Three of the four sequences end with longer phrases than any other phrase in the eight measures. Measures 17 through 24 actually end on the first beat of measure 23 and Miles uses measure 24 to introduce 25. But to further recognize design in this solo one must see the consistent reappearance of three. The pickup begins with the aforementioned two three-note statements. There are two notes connecting the pickup with the next six notes, which are heard in multiples of three two's, including the last note of measure 1 and the first quarter note in measure 2 and the two sets of neighboring notes in between. Beginning with measure 5, there are three three-note groupings which end with the quarter note in measure 6. One could plot out the whole improvisation and see the three pattern emerging throughout. During this period of his career, Miles worked away at a piece, and the other ramifications of this solo demonstrate his methodical mind. The highest notes he plays are a" in measure 5 and a♭" in measure 27. Both of these notes are preceded by rests, the longest rests of the solo, in fact, each lasting 5⅛ beats. This plodding way of doing things seems to indicate that Miles was not quite confident, so he had to be careful. And his playing here was very careful. "Godchild" is one of the few pieces in which Miles uses even a partial phrase from another tune in his improvisation. From the beginning of the first measure to the first quarter note in the second measure, it sounds as if Miles is playing the Jerome Kern song "Bill." But he is never serious about the line, as, throughout this career, he threw out fragments of tunes from time to time. And they remain just that, fragments.

During this early period, his tone—not yet matured—didn't sound forceful, let alone aggressive. He made no attempt to alter the sound of the tones, so, essentially, they all sound the same. That's why these sessions were so valuable to Miles. He had a lot of sound around him so he didn't have to stretch out, which he obviously wasn't ready to do. If the improvisations had been longer, his playing might have sounded monotonous, although his rhythmic development was solid and could have carried him through. On "Godchild," he takes his time, rests when the phrase is down, and seems intent on connecting phrases and giving the piece a clean shot. Not all of the pieces are as well-paced as this one. On the sluggish "Boplicity," which is over-arranged, he moves very timidly at the same snail's pace as the arrangement. On "Budo," he seems rushed, and, instead of articulating, he falls into that muttering sound he had so often as a young musician. On Denzil Best's "Move," his playing is forced, committed to a long phrase at the end which almost makes him run out of air. But on the medium tempo pieces he lays back and, dialoguing with himself, plays beautiful sequential lines. In spite of criticisms of Miles's technique (and he is not now and never has been a virtuoso), he does have a knack for making twists and turns on his instrument which, coupled with his great knowledge of harmony supported by a fantastic ear, allowed him to dart and move either with the band or away from it. However, on "Boplicity," he loses the progressions early and quickly lays out, because the piece is very unsynchronized, with too many disjunct parts.

"Rocker," recorded at the last session on March 9,

1950, finds Miles at one of his best moments of the three sessions. He springs off the line as aggressively as on any of the compositions. Again it is another short solo lasting only one chorus, but, as on most of the pieces, he makes the most of the space he has. One of the important things to remember about all of these sessions is that Miles knew the music beforehand and, when it came time to play, he was on top of the execution of it. Since execution of the written music took precedence at these sessions, Miles agreed to have short solos by everyone to enhance the sound he was trying to create. When he began solos like the one on "Rocker," he knew they had to be concise. But on this particular piece it is obvious that Miles just got started when it was time for Konitz to play a little bit of his lightweight stuff. In spite of what seems to be almost a cutoff, it is apparent that the objective is the sound, because Miles moves over so easily to allow Konitz to begin. What occurred in these sessions was a hint at Miles's abilities, his conciseness, and his realization of what he wanted for himself at this time, fitting his improvisations into a structure which he saw as important to himself. More than anything else, these dates exemplified his intensity and his concentration on what the music was doing and how he could use it to his advantage. It is really impossible to make a lengthy appraisal based on these compositions; at twenty-three, his age when the sessions began (he was almost twenty-four when they ended), he was more competent than when he had been with Parker, and was still very much growing.

"Jeru" (see Appendix), recorded at the first session, was written by baritone saxophonist Gerry Mulligan and has a distinctive call-and-response sound. The piece lasts a total of two minutes and twenty-seven seconds, with Miles's solo lasting approximately forty seconds. So, in that short period of time, there really isn't any way of estimating what his musical personality might be, but there are some indications of how he calculated his solos in listening to how he moved into this one and the others in these sessions. This solo also is one chorus and ranges over two octaves. Miles judiciously utilizes his space by playing his highest note after the longest rest and at the beginning of the second half of his solo (measure 17). Prominent, however, is his gift for duration. Whereas the other players have very little interest in the rhythmic phrases they put together, Miles's ability to put himself into difficult phrase accentuation situations and the consistency with which he complements himself by negotiating these situations strongly characterize his measure as a musician. The triplet in measure 11 serves to point to the second half of the solo, which is predominated by triplets. Miles uses the rests more for breaks in his statements than to organize his breathing. First he plays straight tempo, then a series in which the rests fall on different beats of the measure, producing beautiful syncopation. He has almost mastered space problems, and only occasionally, as in "Move," does he commit himself to playing time lines. It is at these moments when his performance is pushed and one feels that he is struggling. His tone here, not at its best, becomes more spitting when Miles plays *on* tempo, which he seems more inclined to do on up-tempo pieces.

Of all the pieces, "Move" (see Appendix) most clearly shows some of Miles's problems. Besides the ending mentioned before, to which Miles moved with frenzy, the beginning of this improvisation is uncertain. Miles is not quite sure which note he wants to play, so the first one sounds as if it is being squeezed out of the horn. Then he gets into a running staccato pattern from which he never recovers, culminating in the eight-bar eighth-note run, and gasping by the end (from bar 21 to 28). This running staccato playing, on the tempo, dominated his early improvisations but never enhanced his style. He had to work hard to coordinate what he thought he should be playing and what he could play. This discipline shaped his style and his ingenuity, integrating knowledge of harmony, an excellent ear, and a feeling for space. Miles has always been an honest player, rarely taking from others in his improvisations. This collection, *Birth of the Cool*, of more than a year's recording, which is a long time, presents Miles as a young musician fortunate enough to be able to record his early music. There is some real question of the validity of this music because of the length of the solos and the heavy harmonic commitment. Certainly one chorus per piece is no criterion for assessing a man's abilities, but Miles has always played for short periods, and at least his maneuverability in this situation is impressive.

The Capitol sessions more than anything else established Miles as a leader. In the ensemble work, his playing is very strong, and in spite of its shortcomings, his solo playing is much stronger than any of the other soloing on the dates. He contributed "Deception" and collaborated with Bud Powell on "Budo." The latter piece, recorded in the first session, has a brief introduction and a standard A-A-B-A form and is very boppish in its melodic line, with a dialogue construction. "Deception," recorded at the last session and aptly named, finds Miles trying to fit what seems to be every line he ever heard into one composition. There are eight parts, A-B-C-B-C-D-E-C, and just when you feel the improvisations are about to begin, another part appears. Although the improvisations are off balance because of the many chord changes and half-tempo parts, perhaps Miles was trying to do something new with this piece; perhaps it was a testimony to a sound he heard and, along with some other musicians, helped put together.

Miles's style remained static for the next several years. He continued to explore the middle register; as his health deteriorated, the challenge of music made him only more disciplined. His tone improved, sounding more resilient. This was directly attributable to his patience and developing confidence in the *modus operandi* he had manifested through his technical inability; this inability shows up in the Capitol sessions but, in less than a year, is considerably overcome at the early 1951 recording dates with Sonny Rollins. The period between the last Capitol date and 1954 was a tremendous growing time for Miles. Often desperate, through it he became more determined to keep at his music. Although he seemed to be stationary, he had found his style and was slowly perfecting it. In his own composition from this time, a twenty-four-bar blues entitled "Down," the quality of his tone is much fuller than earlier. No longer does that spitting exasperation come through; rather, he has produced a dialogue, now very articulate, between himself and the trumpet. In the language of the people, the word "down" at that time meant what the word "hip" means now. This blues rolls out four eighth notes and a quarter note, with accents on the second, fourth, and first beats of two measures, answered immediately by a dotted quarter note, an eighth note, and another quarter note. As was his custom at this time, Miles takes only a one-chorus solo, with a range of an octave and a major seventh, from a^b to g''. But most interesting in the improvisation is the structure of the rhythmic phrases. Every phrase is answered by the following one, and the patterned placement of notes in the melodic line becomes less important. It is curious that in most of the writings on African-American music, this affiliation with rhythm is overlooked because of a preoccupation with melody and harmony. Miles, negatively appraised in this period for his poor tone and lack of technique, has always had his genius with rhythmic phrases underestimated. At the beginning of his career, over a period including this time, these shapes carried him through and indicated to his contemporaries that he had a spark of something important. On "Down" (see Appendix), his tone is not too encouraging, first gathering strength, then faltering (obviously still reaching for the f'' in measure 24), and often blurring notes, primarily in the lower and higher registers. His melodic lines mostly outline chords or move stepwise to notes. He never moves faster than the tempo, something that Dizzy Gillespie did constantly. Although his playing is still very cautious, Miles uses all his techniques to carve out his phrases, making it sound as if he were telling a story with this arrangement of phrases spewed into the air on a dull voice. Ironically, as was true of Thelonious Monk, the very simplicity of Miles's playing endeared him to the people.

Miles was the first trumpet player to take the lead in the music without using raw strength to overpower it. His approach became more subtle, meticulously working in the middle register, cunningly creating rhythmic patterns by changing accents, expanding and decreasing said pattern sizes, syncopating, and having a certain ongoing conversation with his listeners. His skill began getting sharper as he mastered his area. He wasn't a mature musician when he began recording and leading his own bands, but he became practiced as he worked, and as he worked, his facilities began to grow. He managed to return home to St. Louis and rest occasionally, which certainly helped him deal with some of his elementary problems, but his musicianship straightened itself out on the bandstand. The constant pressure to perform, with Miles always playing with the very best support he could get, began to prove its merits in the beginning of 1953; it was at about this time that out of his diligence emerged a strong voice. His written material was a combination of traditional pop standards like "I Waited for You" and "When Lights Are Low," with lines written at the studios. He not only mastered the middle register but also began to exploit it with sudden bursts and scale runs in up-tempos, something unheard in his earlier playing. Every once in a while, one could hear a slight vibrato, which had started in his early 1950's playing. Perhaps most important was that his tone was no longer suspect and he had stylized his sound, unique to himself. He had gained confidence in his musical mind and saw that his instrument was yielding to his patience and concentration. His followers no longer had to hold their breath, wondering whether he would be able to negotiate an improvisation by hitting the notes squarely or whether he would run out of breath in the middle of a phrase. Occasionally he added the mute, but he wasn't really serious about it at this time.

For the first time in his career Miles knew he could play the instrument, so now he could deal with the music inside his head in a very resolute manner. His contemporaries reassured him by their attention to his music and he became *the* New York musician to see and to play with. He had become a superb medium-tempo player and emphasized the lower register, as other trumpeters showed their skill in the higher register. He worked mostly with a rhythm section that included pianist Horace Silver, bassist Percy Heath, and either Kenny Clarke or Art Blakey on percussion. Silver and Heath were especially effective because Heath had such an excellent ear and kept great tempo and Silver was one of the most superior accompanists ever to play this music, in effect, simply a demon behind Miles. Silver had knowledge of chord structures, in all their inversions and alterations, along with an uncanny ability to play the right chord at the right time, allowing him to back up with a rhythm that seemed to fit perfectly with what Miles and Percy were doing. Heath was one of the first bassists to play duets with Miles with the piano laying out. Miles had great confidence in his playing because Heath was a solid and, most of all, dependable bassist.

On March 6, 1954, Miles recorded what had to be his most impressive collection of pieces of his existing career. Backed by Heath, Silver, and Blakey on a series of compositions that included Monk's "Well You Needn't" and four of his own compositions, along with the standard "It Never Entered My Mind," he demonstrated that his playing had grown by leaps and bounds, and his use of the mute was the most imaginative since "Red" Allen. The mute served more to highlight his style, which was now fixed in the middle and lower registers, giving the music that brooding mood for which he was now becoming famous. His playing on the up-tempo "The Leap" and "Take-Off" was in that classic manner which he had so often mentioned, under the tempo, allowing the piece to be as fast as it was going to be by playing in it, not along with it. With this decision, Miles was able to transform the trumpet, which had long been synonymous with on-the-tempo playing, into a more flexible instrument, unique unto itself. The fact becomes more remarkable when it is recalled that Miles made these adjustments in his use of the instrument to accommodate his own early deficiencies.

In this collection, Miles excelled on the walking-tempo pieces, "Weirdo," "Lazy Susan," and "Well You Needn't." They are predominantly played in the middle range in his methodical way of working phrase after phrase, listening very intently to Silver and Heath and playing off their accompaniment. In his early playing, Miles was so involved with negotiating his ideas with a faltering technique that the interplay between himself and the rhythm was matter of fact. He fully realizes the potential of the rhythm section in "Walkin'," recorded April 29, 1954, and on "Solar," recorded April 3, 1954. They are two of the longest pieces he had recorded up until this time; that is, his improvisations are the longest in terms of the number of choruses on a given set of progressions. His solo on "Walkin'" is 86 measures, seven choruses, and "Solar" has 48 measures, four choruses. On the latter piece he plays his first muted solo with the bass and percussion only, which is absolutely splendid. He bandies with Silver throughout, taking accompanying rhythmic phrases and making them a part of both his solo and the general conversation they have on both pieces.

"Walkin'" (see transcription) is a landmark in

Miles's career. It represents the best playing in this particular period of his evolving style. The people he chose to play with, Lucky Thompson, J. J. Johnson, Silver, Heath, and Clarke, were all in the vanguard of the music. This is not to say that he had solved every one of the problems with his technique, but he did play with great authority. And not enough can be said about the contributions Heath and Silver made to his solo. Miles makes several noticeable mistakes: the lay-back in measure 6 and the smears in measures 39 and 52, all caused by mechanical problems but used well to his advantage. But these things seem insignificant in relation to the ingenuity evinced by his improvisation. His proficient use of changing rhythm patterns, which sometimes gets him into trouble and causes the occasional *faux pas,* is strengthened by both his anticipation of the accompanying players and his ability to build his phrases on theirs. An example is the phrase beginning at measure 16 and ending at measure 18, the same phrase heard from Silver in measure 15. It is also interesting that he uses a series of triplets only twice, although it seems to be more often. Starting at measure 26 and going all the way to the fourth beat in measure 36, almost a whole chorus dominated by triplet figures occurs. In fact, it is a whole chorus if one counts the pickup in measure 25 and the whole measure rest beginning in measure 36. The next time triplets are used is from measure 70 through 72, and because of the accents Miles uses, they sound completely different. He often prepares his listener for what's coming next by playing a fragment of it; for instance, he begins the only series of four connected sixteenth notes, an often-used phrase in African-American music, by announcing it two bars earlier (the fragment occurs at bar 43 and the uninterrupted sixteenths begin on the last beat of measure 45). The first triplet phrase, mentioned previously, is Miles's response to hearing Silver's triplet just before. The triplet figure was one of Horace's favorite devices in his accompaniment, so by this time Miles was used to hearing it and was probably looking for it. His patience in dipping, weaving, and mixing the phrases while always talking and listening to his accompaniment are the kind of nuances that carried him to this date and are most prominent in it.

"Walkin' " is a twelve-bar blues with an eight-bar introduction. Miles's solo stays almost exclusively in the middle register, having a range of only an octave and a seventh beginning at a^b and going to a". His playing progresses up and down, with the widest skip being an octave and only occurring once. His next biggest jump is a seventh, done once, and then a minor sixth, which also occurs once. Most of the jumps are fifths, fourths, thirds, and smaller. This is by no means a chromatic solo; but his use of close intervals reminds one of his early training in the chromatic scale. By this time, Miles had worked diligently on the intervals in the half valves and was beginning to incorporate those sounds into his playing. The solo uses very few accidentals and harmonically hovers around F, B^b, and B^b minor; again, he uses this all-important juxtaposition of major and minor. The line of the solo moves mainly up and down, only occasionally changing direction in a phrase before it hits the bottom note; Miles usually plays down registers at this time, using the upper to highlight, but that not too seriously. It really is a credit to Miles's genius that he was able to develop a style which exploited his weaknesses. This style, still evolving, took full advantage of his strength, the middle register, and his ability to connect rhythmic phrases into a dialogue, and forged his mistakes into a positive result.

"Walkin'" really established Miles. The longest improvisation on record to that date, it best represented what he was doing in public. The consistent gap between recorded material and the material played in public has always been a serious problem for recording musicians of African-American music. The record companies control the material in the studio, so most African-American artists always sound better in person. Miles achieved this sound using traditional material, a standard twelve-bar blues played in medium tempo. His solo laid out hard bop, and he underscored the tradition of the music, rhythm, with this beautiful articulation.

His March 6th recording of "It Never Entered My Mind" was the first recording on which he used mute as a leader. Since Miles stays very close to the line during his solo, it should be considered a rendition rather than an improvisation. The piece begins with a two-bar arpeggio introduction by Silver which he continues when Miles starts the melody, playing slow staccato notes (M.M. $\quad = 66$), that elegantly combine with the arpeggio. During all this, Heath is playing on the beat, which, in combination with them, immediately sets up three rhythmic patterns: two strict and Miles's syncopated. Miles's playing merely embellishes the melody rather than working on a set of chord progressions. His use of the mute has always been effective, even though here there is a slight hiss coming through which gives his tone a dragging sound. He prefers to be cautious with the mute, as was always his way when turning to a new mechanism on record.

"Solar," recorded less than a month later, was a

stunning improvement, especially in confidence. All of the April 3rd pieces were with the mute and they varied in tempo from the slow "You Don't Know What Love Is" (M.M. $\quad = 48$) to the medium-tempo "Solar" (M.M. $\quad = 168$) to the up-tempo "Love Me or Leave Me" and "I'll Remember April " (M.M. $\quad = 208$ *ca.*). Each has its own flavor, and from his solos on "Solar" and "You Don't Know What Love Is," he began to develop a reputation as a lyrical player. This reputation has some validity, because these two compositions are really sung, but he goes beyond lyricism to use the song concept in a different vein. His playing is still without vibrato, not attempting to incorporate the pure sound which is usually associated with a lyrical sound. Miles, doing what he learned so carefully from Parker, used the progression of a piece to carve out his own series of melodic lines, still in that very unique dialogue. Though he stayed close to the line on "It Never Entered My Mind," "You Don't Know What Love Is" is swiftly carried from away the written line by the beautiful use of embellishments. The piece is an indication of his strong knowledge of harmony and his creative way of developing long connecting lines. He used the instrument as it had not been used before, mostly to cancel his deficiences, playing the middle register exclusively on medium- and slow-tempo pieces with a richness and individualization of sound that would change the concepts of how to deal with the trumpet. He was using the mute as much as any of his contemporaries and twice as effectively. This is not to say that he had no room to grow, but that he had developed his style so finely that he could play anything he wanted.

Miles's mute sound is soft, and on the ballads, it

seems as if he is giving every note special consideration. "You Don't Know What Love Is" is carried out meticulously, changing major and minor figures while as attentive to Silver's accompaniment as if it were leading him through the maze of his mind. Percy negotiates the whole piece, with its changing rhythmic and harmonic patterns, in his usual flawless manner, playing mainly low on the fingerboard until Miles plays a short part in double-time, when he then plays higher on the board to give a lighter feeling. Most interesting in this piece are the interval relationships and the rhapsodic feeling conveyed by them. Miles will play a two-note major phrase, then a short run to a two-note minor or diminished phrase; he is constantly moving the composition away from and back to the line, with the progressions very meaningful but the line having little importance beyond being something to toy with. Silver and Heath play very close lines moving together, allowing Miles to wander and weave at will. There is no limit to the praise that Heath and Silver should receive for the work they did behind Miles. Not only were they steady and always dependable, but their accompaniment was extremely creative, always moving, shifting, and giving Miles a constant variety of sounds to which to respond. They were the first of a long line of brilliant rhythm section people that Miles would employ.

"Solar" was the only composition by Miles played on this date, and it fit his style very comfortably. It is a series of answering phrases in a twenty-four-bar form. He plays mostly eighth notes and no triplets, which gives the straight-on feeling the piece projects. Heath is doubly dangerous on this piece, holding the tempo with only an intermittent syncopation. His intonation, as always, is impeccable. If a heart ever needed a pacer, then Heath's pulse would more than take care of business. It was not only his time but also his note selection, moving up and down the strings, knowing all the stops, making all the right chord substitutions, moving to significant chord changes by half-steps, and creating a whole, round tone, that stamped this towering bassist. Miles, who understands more than most about together musicianship, used this piece to play his first recorded piano lay-out chorus. Percy responds with a non-syncopated line that, along with Miles's, creates one of the finest example of mixed rhythm counterpoint (fifth species) one would ever want to hear. It's the way Percy moves through the progression, playing strictly on the beat, that produces his very fine melodic pattern. Beginning with measure 15 when Miles is resting, Percy enters the measure playing a line which is going up a minor third, down a minor second, up a minor third, down a major second, up a major third, down a minor third, and up a minor third which he sequences in a higher octave. This movement heightens Miles's entry in the second half of measure 15 and into the end of the solo and is just one of the many outstanding contributions Percy makes to this music.

Miles concentrates very hard on this piece, with nothing at all fancy but a consistently developed, straight line. Of the seventy-two bars of improvisation, only one measure repeats itself in measures 9 and 10 of his second improvisation. He mixes the rhythmic phrases very well, although he does show an affinity for the half-measure phrase of a dotted eighth note followed by a sixteenth repeated. This particular figure appears thirty-one times and, by the end of the second improvisation, you know you've heard it. The range is

still in the middle, $a^{b\prime\prime}$ the highest note and middle C'
the lowest, with Miles making few wide jumps but
using major and minor interlockings beautifully. Again,
the movement of his solo is as the piece is structured,
going down the staff. The line of the piece opens with
an establishment ot B^b which is transposed down a
minor third, stabilizing A^b, with the solo taking the
same trend. The middle C, the lowest note, is played
nine times whereas the highest note, the $a^{b\prime\prime}$, is played
only twice. With his fantastic ear, Miles utilizes space
brilliantly, with accents falling all over the place. In
the pace of "Solar," no other trumpet player, outside
of Clifford Brown, worked as diligently and used his
support to its maximum. "Solar" opens with Silver and
Heath playing one chord (D-E^b-G-B-G+5), after which
Heath and Miles enter on the second half of the second
beat of the measure; when Miles begins his second improvisation, that same chord is played by Silver with
Miles beginning his solo on the same beat. Such is the
symmetrical mind of Miles Davis, and it only made
good sense to be as creative as possible when in the
company of such outstanding support. Miles, formally
adding the mute, a new aspect of his playing, took advantage of the situation. Kenny Clarke, playing brushes
throughout the session, was brisk and particularly effective as another voice when Percy and Miles played
together without Silver. He always kept the pace up,
never letting it drag, so he and Percy complemented one
another within the unity.

Miles had spent ten years in New York and his
style seemed to be settling in, strong in the middle,
with imaginative rhythms and a dialoguing tone that
defied description and only recently had become legit-
imate. No one else was doing what he was doing on

the trumpet. It was clear that he was influencing younger trumpeters, Donald Byrd in particular, and that he was bringing a new sample of lyricism to the music, one that sang lines but with an ironical, biting tonal quality. He was thrown into the competitive popularity polls with Clifford Brown, but they really were very different players, so to compare them would not result in a better understanding of Miles. Miles was still playing eighth notes, not dealing with tempo too much within the structure of a piece and not playing too many up-tempo pieces. He sounds slightly rushed on "Blue 'n' Boogie" (April 29) and the two up-tempo compositions on April 3rd. His forte was the infinite variety of rhythmic patterns and, in combination· with his knowledge of numbers, he had established alternative avenues for dealing with music. There is always the tendency to believe that a musician has his solo mapped out at the onset, and that might be true of a person who is always playing the same thing, but to an artist like Davis only the symmetry of the piece is there, so strongly that the parts must fall into place. Miles only had the progressions and a limited facility to work with, so it is what he did with them that won him the admiration of his contemporaries. His mute just added to the mystery of the manner in which he approached the instrument, down register instead of up. It was another way of stamping his style—a way of making him unique by demonstrating a different way of playing the trumpet. The abundance of musical ideas inside him permitted Miles to overcome his shortcomings and to pioneer in trumpet playing.

All of this development came before Miles managed a band of his own. Now that he had become *the* musician to play with, it was time for him to select a wise musician partner for the numerous gigs he was beginning to get. He wanted another horn, someone to stimulate his own playing, so he first picked Sonny Rollins. But Rollins with his strong melodic and lay-back playing was too close to Miles's own style, so it was fortunate that he decided to play with the Max Roach/Clifford Brown band instead of Miles's band. By the middle of 1955, Miles had picked two-thirds of his first permanent rhythm section: one Philadelphian, "Philly" Joe Jones, on percussion and "Red" Garland, from Dallas, Texas, on piano. By the autumn of that year he had selected the full band, adding bassist Paul Chambers and tenor saxophonist John Coltrane. There were lots of outstanding rhythm sections around, Art Blakey with bassist Doug Watkins and pianist Silver, Richie Powell with Max Roach and bassist George Morrow, but none had the overall spark that this group had. It was unquestionably the most aggressive band around and Chambers and Jones really made Miles play. They were two revolutionary players and Miles's overall style changed in their company. He was playing faster and seemed more comfortable with up-tempo pieces, which this band executed with masterful au-thority. He began to play in the higher register more often and became far less cautious than he had been a year before. He continued to duet with the bass with-out piano in the style he had begun with Percy Heath, strongly indicating the confidence he had in the young bassist Chambers. On the October 27, 1955, recording of "S'posin'" Chambers makes the bass hum behind Miles's playing. He had great control, could play any tempo, had superior note selection, and combined the strong tempo qualities of Heath with the linear rhyth-mic lines of Charles Mingus. He was an imaginative improviser who combined pizzicato with arco in an equally dextrous fashion. Philly Joe received the same abuse from critics that Elvin Jones would receive later when he first started playing with Trane—too loud, too complex. He drove this band, and his mixing of rhythms probably played a large part in Trane's hiring of Elvin, because John Coltrane really expanded in Miles's setting. Garland gave Miles the solid harmonic support he wanted from a pianist, and he was a far superior soloist to Silver. It was Chambers and Jones who wound up this band and propelled it. With their unfailing support, Miles and Trane grew and grew in a relationship that was more reciprocal than most thought.

It is difficult to estimate potential for growth, but the energy that was present on the bandstand every night when these five musicians played was enormous. Miles watched Trane blossom right before his eyes, and Miles's playing became more different from the norm than it already was. He had now begun to put that stylized tone into rapid-fire rhythmic phrases, and his intensity penetrated the people and reached out to grab minds. It was like playing with Parker again but a hundred times improved in Miles's own right and still gettin' up. On a date with Mingus earlier in the year, he had demonstrated that he had mastered what he was then doing, so it was time to move, because he wasn't ready to be contented. When he hired this new rhythm section and Trane, Miles knew that it wouldn't be about slouching. The music they played was as free and flexible as any Miles had ever played. There were always changes in the tempos of pieces they played, something that Miles had stayed away from in his earlier music. He rode this section so well, playing on the tempo, halving it, doubling it, and always in that talking, communicating exchange of statements by using scores of sequences, expanding and decreasing rhythmic figures, and now expanding his range possibilities. Miles and Trane, listening to one another night after night and fired up by the most potent rhythm section around then, just couldn't help expand their horizons. One of the long-held fallacies about this music had been that, if two strong musical spirits were put together, their temperaments would naturally create animosity. This certainly happens, but if a musician feels the need to play the best he possibly can, then having another inspirational spirit beside him only perks up that need. Miles continued to grow in the next several years, with a noticeable improvement in his playing right after he formed his quintet.

Miles's style itself was not changing much any longer, but he was now constantly refining it. He was still predominantly a middle-register player, not because he was unable to play the high register, but because he heard the music there. His voice was still staccato in its movement and he seemed slightly uneasy in up-tempos, but he had learned not to panic and force lines, which had caused early problems, but to play implied times and allow the rhythm section to carry the tempo while he played around it. He had always played that way anyhow, so now he was begining to control it with all tempos, staying away from any phrase which made him sound as if he were straining on the toilet. His improvisations continued to be very economical although he had substantially increased the number of choruses he would take on any given set of progressions. Refining what he had and where he heard music was the next stage of his personal evolution. Equally important was the fact that, in his first real band, he had hired three genuinely revolutionary musicians—nothing hampered their progress. In making an assessment of African-American music, the musical associates of an individual player are usually an excellent barometer of where he sees the music heading.

As Miles had added the mute to give his voice another sound, so he added the flügelhorn to exploit further the possibilities of his area of musical concentration. It was a specialty horn, and his uses of it got him the job for the *Music for Brass* date in the fall of 1956. He played the flügelhorn with a heavy sound, as he did the trumpet. Miles's facile movement on the trumpet has always disguised the heaviness of his sound, but it is this weight that produces the penetration. When Miles plays constantly changing patterns, one doesn't feel this weight so much, but it is obvious that one of the things he had to work on eliminating while growing through his horn was the heavy sound which had developed while he was getting rid of the bothersome spitting. Miles is aware of all the mechanisms which could affect his sound during a performance, knowing how to use the acoustics of a hall, the microphone, and all the things present to enhance his sound. The flügelhorn fit in perfectly with his voice, and his real seriousness about the horn emerged on the dates he made in the middle of 1957, called *Miles Ahead*.

Miles had a significant enough interest in the sound of the larger orchestra to put some of his energy into playing in that situation, the results of which were undeniably excellent. The flügelhorn was just another strong testimony to his fine inner ear and an indication of the range in which he heard himself. His playing on these four dates was unusually strong, especially because he was working exclusively with the new instrument. It was obvious that the low range and the mellowness of the instrument fit his expression perfectly. He also demonstrated a new dexterity which found him articulating more clearly than most times in the past. The structure of these dates enabled Miles to do what he does best, to weave, turn, mix phrases rhythmically, enter and exit as the only soloist, with the band acting as his accompanist. He waited almost ten years to do this again, and the relaxed way in which he plays, evinced in all of the pieces on *Miles Ahead,* speaks to his pleasure in doing the full orchestra. During these takes, he is in and out of the ensemble numerous times. He does more than one would expect the leader of an orchestra to do in terms of ensemble playing, but he manages to enhance his own playing by constantly leaping in and out of the solo and the ensemble. Miles plays using short phrases, getting strong support from the arrangements, and this setting is ideal. Miles is just reaffirming his flexibility. He gets along just as well playing with only the bass and percussion on long polyphonic lines as with the twenty-one-piece orchestra. Making better music had become the major preoccupation of Miles Davis.

All of this indicates the transformation he was going through in the company of his band. He was forced to be even more diligent than before in order to deal with the talent in the new group. For a musician like Miles, it was challenging to come to the realization that he must technically master the instrument, which he literally did, just to maintain a balance with the creativity of the rest of the band. The *Miles Ahead* compositions underscored the remarkable improvement now obvious in his technique. His ideas were able to flow because of his greater proficiency, as he burst out lines he had only recently learned to negotiate. Ironically, though he had progressed significantly in his ability to get over the instrument, his style had changed very little because he already knew where he wanted to play, not regarding music as the acrobatic challenge that it was to many other trumpeters.

On the take "Springsville" (see transcription), which is up-tempo (M.M. $\downarrow$ = 208 ca.), Miles displays all his honed skills. He mixes his phrases again with as much variety as ever but now uses more vibrato, and quite a noticeable one. His rhythmic phrases are in faster times, and he is doing more scalar runs than he had previously. Examining his melodic patterns closely, one finds they take the same shape they have always taken, but now his vastly improved technique allows him to be more sophisticated in the accents. The strong aspect of his whole style is the communicative way he organizes his rhythmic shapes, the fact that each phrase always answers the one before it. In some ways, he is still conservative; he rarely runs to a high note but rather uses his rest to prepare for them. An example of the latter is the e" which begins the final chorus, prepared for not only by the rest but also by the orchestra's moving more and more up the staff during Miles's rest. The striking thing about this entire collection, and Miles's further development, is the singing quality in his voice. Miles's sound has more of a human quality than perhaps any trumpeter who has played this music. Now he was adding a slight vibrato, playing more long notes, especially in the slow numbers which, from him, were now becoming ballads. Miles has always repeated many melodic phrases during the course of a single improvisation, usually with slight variations or changes in context. The beautiful "Blues for Pablo," by Gil Evans, really demonstrates this newfound lyricism; he sings in that blues voice in which two of his notes suddenly become more significant than two hundred of anyone else's. But what was unmistakably happening in these sessions was a conscious effort to create a total sound. In his Capitol venture, the band wasn't built solely around him but around other soloists as well. Now he is by himself. He dances through a series of splendid arrangements, which cover the few flaws of his playing, giving each piece enough individuality to keep them all from sounding alike. This time there was only one arranger, Gil Evans, and Miles was in close contact with him every step of the way, so he really knew the music.

The expansion of the band from a quintet to a sextet, by the return of Trane to augment Cannonball (who had himself replaced Trane earlier), really accelerated the music in the band. Miles had something special on his hands now. They certainly tested his mettle, since he insisted on playing in very high tempos, and the recordings became very different from what was happening in live performances. The energy being put forth by their collaboration every night, augmented by the fact that Miles was allowing Cannonball and Trane to play as they wished, resulted in one of the most revolutionary bands of the late fifties. Miles was actually playing too fast, often getting so caught up by a rapid, twisting phrase that it caused a breakdown and forcing of his sound. It was at this time that he began to stumble through phrases and his tone reverted to some of its old growls. Trying to compensate somehow, he moved to the modal music, which he hoped would give space to work and also allow maximum freedom for Cannonball and Trane. His public performances mixed old standards with the new music based mainly on modes. Modal music permits a player to conform to a tonic rather than a series of harmonic progressions. In a thirty-two-bar blues, a player could improvise on one tonic for sixteen bars and move to another for the next sixteen, allowing for more freedom and less complicated chordal movement. Of course this helped Trane and Cannonball in one way, but the music became lethargic because the change to modal music decelerated the tempos; although this was fine for Miles, it debilitated the raw power of Coltrane. Garland and Philly Joe had left the band before Miles decided on modality, so this move was probably instigated more by pianist Bill Evans, who entered the band in late spring of 1958.

It is interesting at least to compare Miles in the different sextets, first with Garland and Philly Joe and then in the one manned by Bill Evans and Jimmy Cobb. On April 2 and 3, 1958, Miles completed takes that included "Two Bass Hit," the 1940's classic written by John Lewis and Dizzy Gillespie, Thelonious Monk's "Straight, No Chaser," the young saxophonist Jackie McLean's "Dr. Jekyll," the old standard "Billy Boy," played by the rhythm section, and two pieces by Miles, "Sid's Ahead," which first appeared in 1954 as "Weirdo," and "Milestones." The compositions themselves show the great versatility of the band. For a soloist leader to feature the rhythm section doing its own cut was virtually unknown; it attested to Miles's respect for the other members. The material also demonstrated the band's commitment to the music they had grown up with, which, first and foremost, swung. In their way, they made it a tribute to their brothers and gave them a short share of the royalties; it is really unbelievable that while African-Americans have created all this great music, we seldom support each other by playing one another's compositions. The tempos here range from the very high-tempo "Two Bass Hit" to the up-tempo "Straight, No Chaser," another up-tempo, "Dr. Jekyll," to the medium up-tempo "Milestones," and finally to the walking blues "Sid's Ahead." The overall sound is fresh and crisp, as if it just came out of the oven. Juxtaposing Miles and Coltrane brings out their similarities, as the proximity of Miles and Parker highlights their likenesses. Miles mainly plays on the beat and, on the up-tempos, plays around and within the tempo, but rarely on it. Most of the time, Trane is playing as fast as he can, obliterating the melodic line and trying to take the progressions away, but the rhythm section is holding too tough to allow it. Trane is playing much longer lines here, and a tally of the numerous thirty-second and sixty-fourth-note phrases would show what his playing was about in 1958. Their styles were so different, yet listening more closely proves Miles was very well teamed up with Chambers, since by this time, they had developed a great reciprocal anticipatory feeling. Coltrane was relating more to the multidirectional rhythms of Philly Joe, while Garland was adding some spice at the most appropriate times. Cannonball was playing as well as he has ever played, continually challenging the boundaries of harmony, a far cry from "Mercy, Mercy."

Miles seemed overshadowed by his towering horn sidemen, and, at times, he was; but when he was where he could really operate, they were three equal voices. The twelve-bar minor blues, "Sid's Ahead" (see Appendix), clearly attests to this. Miles begins his solo after Trane's and plays seven choruses, all with Chambers and Philly Joe. This strolling tempo (M.M. $\quad$ = 108) is Miles's forte, ready-made for his style. Each chorus is unique, connected with a last bar half-measure rest, then beginning the next chorus on the last two beats of the last measure. At this time, Miles's musical mind is that symmetrical. Everything seems to be worked out this way, but you hear him responding to Chambers and playing off Chambers' line, so the spontaneity is still there. Chambers, a very different bassist from Percy Heath, was an equally strong pulse player, but one who syncopated more often than he held the pulse. In this tempo, and in just about everything he did with Miles, he enhanced Miles's playing tremendously. Paul was strong anywhere on the bass but was particularly adept at changing octaves at a single bound; he was excellent moving up the bass (through octaves) but had superior sensitivity going down the bass, then exploiting that by moving half-steps up to the next progression. He had a habit of playing patterns that would move by repeating once each note he had used in his accompaniment. It was especially effective. His accompaniment of the trumpet during Miles's first improvisation on "Sid's Ahead" was masterful. If Miles was going up the registers, Chambers would be moving right along with him, suddenly skip to a lower octave, giving the solo a funky street feeling. Each chorus of his accompaniment was different from the preceding one because Miles's was. In the first chorus he skips seven times, glissandos once and just plays everything on time. He keeps in Miles's "cakes" constantly. During Chambers' long tenure with Miles, whatever the tempo was, the lines he played accompanying Miles were

every bit as interesting as what Miles himself was doing. Miles handles "Ahead" in that dialoguing manner
now distinctly his, exploring the middle and lower
registers but moving occasionally and very deliberately
near the high register. His articulation is clear and very
mobile for the number of objectives he has, all of
which he accomplishes cleanly. His melodic line has
become as important as his rhythmic phrase, making
him doubly dangerous. The lines are longer, each more
explicit, usually in six-measure patterns. Like every
great improviser, Miles connects his lines, masterfully
making things meet while perpetually changing directions.

As stunning as this solo is, Miles still sounds very
uncomfortable in the more up-tempo pieces. He plays
only the head on "Two Bass Hit" and is very tight on
"Dr. Jekyll." On the latter, Trane and Ball take it away
after Miles obviously has given it up. "Milestones" and
"Straight, No Chaser" are played beautifully, but, more
importantly, are examples of the potential of this band
put out there for the people to see; it was clear that
Miles had before this time simply accommodated his
talents and skills. But by the end of May, Garland and
Jones were no longer in the band, and in their replacements, Miles was opting for a more lyrical sound, at least
in the piano, and probably all around. On May 26, the
new band, with Evans and Cobb, recorded three pieces
that were a definite departure from the band's usual
repertoire: there were two ballads, "Green Dolphin
Street" and "Stella by Starlight," and an African-American children's folk song, "Put Your Little Foot Right
Out." The three were taken at very slow tempos, and
the long solo at the beginning of "Green Dolphin Street"
was used to introduce Bill Evans and to indicate things

to come—that is, Miles would play more mute on more ballads. Further evidence of this new movement occurred at the 1958 Newport Jazz Festival, where Miles played short solos and not at all on "Two Bass Hit," and Evans just accompanied, except for "Fran Dance" and "Straight, No Chaser." It was clear that in public performances where the tempos were sky-high, Coltrane and Adderley were carrying the weight. But the time for redemption was coming as, in that same month of July, Miles began the recordings for *Porgy and Bess.*

Porgy and Bess was the culmination of Miles's effort in the medium of the large orchestra. It was unquestionably this album that convinced Columbia that they had a major talent, both by artistry and sales. It found Miles playing trumpet and flügelhorn and fusing with Gil Evans to produce a most profound performance of traditional material. As in most of Miles's interpretations of a given piece, the arrangements were only skeletons of the original material. Miles has always done his creating right on the spot, although it is thought out for a long time in advance. The music is played with passion and outright love for the sound, as, through Miles, the spirit of African-American people is conveyed. There is something about the history of the music embodied in this spirit which makes them not only arrangements but bits and pieces of things past. The tuba and double bass line which ends "The Buzzard Song" is reminiscent of the fact that the tuba was the predecessor of the double bass. All through the music there are touches of Duke Ellington as well. The execution of the written parts is a superb total effort, especially because there are so many inflections in Evans' music, with parts continually moving in and out.

Many of the arrangements are in faster tempos than in the previous music and the dynamics are more versatile. It's not that the harmonies are so great, because if one listens closely to the voicings, one can hear parts of *Miles Ahead* and the Capitol sessions; but it is the way in which Gil Evans uses them that provides them with a more sophisticated, unique sound. As always, Evans surrounds Miles with sound, darting in and out like tuna trying to stay away from the big catch. Miles's improvisations are longer, and this marks the first time he plays isolated with bass and drums. (As in *Miles Ahead,* there is no piano.) Philly Joe Jones is used for these dates, since Miles wanted more dynamics and felt that Philly Joe could provide the needed power by the way he played his butt off. Miles even gives him a solo on "Gone," and he plays short pieces from take to take; he is very prominent. What has always been underestimated about these sessions is the amount of music that Evans and Miles brought to the dates. It seems that the harder the arrangements are, the better the band plays them. But the lines themselves are extended fragments of Gershwin's lines which, as always for Miles, offer him great movement and flexibility. The pieces swing with exceptional part movement. There are always exchanges of parts from one section to another in Evans/Davis collaborations which, though like a constant chatter, never really detract from the soloists. In fact, everything works to project Miles and to support his improvisations. More important is the fact that Miles had thought about this project for some time, probably talking at length with Evans about how best to use the studio, how all the mechanics would affect the music, and how best to utilize the written music. Thus, the orchestra was very well-rehearsed, and like any artistically successful project, this one was well-planned.

Although Miles had played trumpet and flügelhorn on the *Music for Brass* dates in 1956, this was the first time he combined all his musical components, including the mute. He plays trumpet on "Gone, Gone, Gone," "Prayer," with mute on "Summertime," and on the remainder he plays flügelhorn. His trumpet tone is brighter, with more assurance. The flügelhorn sound is slightly dull, just where Miles wants it to be. His overall playing is not infallible and still seems to be fluttering somewhat here and there, especially since he seems more comfortable with the flügelhorn in this situation. One of the things affecting the reception of Miles's present playing is that, because he was always saddled with a reputation for bad technique, when you hear an error in articulation you just roll with it because it has become a facet of his style. There is still great spirit and tremendous interpretation, but now the mood is turning somewhat rhapsodic. But there is nothing syrupy or superfluous about this effort, since the energy that went into it captured everyone involved. By now Miles's reputation as a musician was attracting other musicians into his circle for the purpose of accomplishing something that required a first-class amount of concentration to carry it off. What Miles did here was break out his best stylized variation of a well-known theme, and, whatever it is imaginable to do with a series of compositions called *Porgy and Bess*, Miles did it. It seems as if his energy authorized this rendition of *Porgy and Bess* to be distinctively Miles Davis'. None of the pieces personifies this more than "Summertime."

Recorded on the last date of the sessions (August 14), "Summertime" (see transcription) is the only piece which uses the muted trumpet. It had always been interpreted as an extremely slow piece, but not here. The interesting thing about this undertaking is the extensive improvisation involved in the effort and, subsequently, the liberties taken on every tune. This music is not impressionistic but expressionistic, trying to express an idea about an idea. Thus the tempo is much faster than usual on "Summertime," and Miles is accompanied by a seven-note motif which continually repeats itself, passing from one section of the orchestra to another. Miles plays five choruses, developing a strophic form by the interplay of soloist and orchestra, reminiscent of the traditional call-and-response in the roots of African-American music. The accompaniment is muted, and the pattern played is altered slightly over the eight measures. The first six measures are relatively the same, and the last two close out each episode. While the congregation is responding with praise, the preacher embellishes the melodic theme, always listening to how the congregation reacts. Here Miles stays close to the melody; that is, there are glimpses of the melody in every chorus. The tempo is the pace Miles relates to best, strolling. His dialogue style always sustains the movement with lines that are never lines for their own sake but for the sake and maintenance of the music. This is especially true when he plays the trumpet. He has better control and range with that instrument, because he hasn't worked out all the mechanical nuances on the flügelhorn. His work on all the takes bears his remarkable stamp, and because Evans understood every aspect of that stamp, Miles was relaxed. He always played well in this kind of setting, and nothing epitomized this more than this series of dates.

Modal music wasn't as much a stylistic change for Miles as it was an attempt to find a vehicle that would utilize both his own talents and those of the other members of the band. In its outward form, and even its application, it could have been an ideal mechanism. It was apparent that the band was able to play in any situation, and the fact that Miles originally pulled this form on them cold clearly indicated the confidence he had in the form itself as well as in the other players. The tempos were very slow, and the music was beautiful but lethargic. Because of this, Coltrane and Cannonball seemed restricted in an outlet that should have given them the greatest of freedom. After Philly Joe left the band, some of the spark and electricity he carried went with him. Jimmy Cobb wasn't nearly the same musical personality, although he does a great job on the July 29th session of *Porgy and Bess*. Miles's playing was far more lyrical than it had ever been, with a stronger singing motif rather than the rhythmic one which had shaped his core of individualism; again his playing was cautious and sometimes almost cute. He had great control over his embouchure, the air streams moving the way he wanted them and lines coming out of his horn, first long and thin but getting bigger and harder and vice versa. His apparently very heavy sound, which no longer had to move chromatically, was taking wide skips, making really interesting melodic lines but sounding as if he could play them in his sleep. His first interest in Spanish music also appeared in his modal approach. "Flamenco Sketches" was among the new lines that were written in this period, which group also included "All Blues" and "So What." The latter one of the pieces that had a great flexibility of tempo. By this time, Bill Evans was in and out of the band, though mostly out, becoming very influential in what was going on. His literate knowledge of music sharpened Miles, and his lyricism, a harmonically complicated manner of improvisation which rarely played well fast, affected Miles quite a bit. "Blue in Green" (see Appendix) really spotlights Evans, not that Miles hadn't provided a showcase for other members of the band, but in this piece his and Coltrane's solos are kept short, seeming to stop before they even get started. Miles is particularly plodding in this piece which both he and Evans wrote. He has always known where he is in terms of his music, never overestimating how his style enhances his music. He knew he had developed in a certain manner which accommodated the treble clef, and he knew, and had known for a long time, that he wasn't comfortable playing at up-tempos, nor was he strong on long improvisations because of the intense way in which he approaches music. Miles was always a teller of tales through his music, so this move toward lyricism, which really had been coming for some time, was more logical to his mind than was first apparent to anyone else.

Except for a brief moment at the outset, Miles pioneered the sixties without either Coltrane or Adderley. The only person left from his original quintet was Paul Chambers, who, like so many other outstanding young musicians before him, stayed with the established band for a while before going off to form his own band. Dating back to Louis Armstrong's debut with the "King" Oliver band, this pattern has recurred. There has never really been any formalized educational institution where people who want to play African-American music can learn and develop their skills. The only source of knowledge has been experience in the bands themselves, especially the working bands; this is where the younger musician has always learned his trade. There are some who believe that this is the best and only natural way, but this is not to say that the practice of our music cannot be better serviced in a place that is more conducive to learning and where some of the ills that have constantly plagued us can be reduced or eliminated.

Miles's first choice to replace his two horn sidemen was Jimmy Heath, who had recently returned from being institutionalized. He played with Miles on a few gigs, and the music was working out fine, but his parole board refused to allow him to travel beyond a ninety-mile-radius of Philadelphia, so he ultimately lost the job. It is absurd and tragic that his rehabilitation should have been hampered by inflexible rules; Heath's unfair treatment greatly disturbed Miles, forcing him to cancel some of his commitments because he suddenly found himself without a horn sideman suitable to his taste. Heath would have been perfect alongside Miles; their personal relationship went back to Miles's admiration of Jimmy's older brother Percy, and then, in 1954, Jimmy had played on successful record dates with Miles. Heath was also an excellent writer and arranger, but this was not to be his time for that. Miles's playing style was fixed now. He had decided where he was best suited and it was apparent that the public agreed with this decision, if popularity is any indication of a man's worth. (In this music it becomes very dubious!)

Sketches of Spain most assuredly demonstrates his mastery of the instrument and his genius in the style that he had selected for himself. He does so many different things on this series of dates, which began at the end of 1959, and finished in March of 1960. He bends and shapes sounds at will, skillfully bringing a new meaning to playing the trumpet. More than anything else, *Sketches* demonstrates how far he had gone with his pensive, brooding style, that he had mastered playing the spaces between the minor intervals, and that his ear was second to none. Because he had finally overcome all his mechanical deficiencies, his sound was no longer hampered by practical errors. A few years earlier, he had arrived at where he wanted to play, and now he could put his full concentration on what he wanted to play. But as *Sketches* shows, Miles fell into the same trap as many other African-American musicians, making European classical music a standard of justification for our music. That standard is quite alien, though it is true that some Europeans, like Rodrigo, a Spanish composer, used native folk music in their works, but it is also true that he was considered just another composer writing in the European classical tradition, certainly not innovative. There is really nothing about *Sketches* which reminds one in any way of African-American music. Tempo and combined rhythms are almost nonexistent, and, as well as Miles plays, it is still slow, methodical, and with a very low energy level. The brainwashing of cultural oppression makes the oppressed person feel, and I mean strongly feel, that the oppressor is essentially correct in his assessment of the victim's culture. And here is Miles, the pillar of individualism, the man most musicians looked up to for his uncompromising stand on music, a person who had overcome obstacle after obstacle, finally submitting to pressure which had, as early as the Capitol sessions, persuaded him that this was the way to go. And it was with this recording, *Sketches,* that he finally acknowledged his victimization.

He was set now. He knew what kind of musicianship he wanted to surround himself with, an excellent rhythm section with a competent horn sideman. His relationship with the new bands was very professional, the arrangements were tight, and the room for improvisation became fixed. His popularity became greater and greater, and he began winning popular polls. But while the music of African-American people became more liberated from the chains of European concepts of harmony and melody, his music seemed more inclined to conform to those guidelines. His music was more beautiful than it was challenging, unlike the innovative decade preceding it. His ballad playing became his hallmark, and his repertoire between 1955 and 1965 changed only slightly. He was becoming more famous for his renditions of "My Funny Valentine" and "Stella by Starlight," in which the bands were absolutely unique and stunning, but they presented nothing new or exciting. Miles had not become commonplace and he wasn't relating to any weird devices—the music just hadn't moved and he was playing where he felt most comfortable. He had become literally the most outstanding player in the hard-bop tradition, a tradition that was still holding on to progressions and, now, established forms. None of this is to claim that he wasn't playing as strongly as he had ever played; in fact, his playing was stronger than ever, but there were no more surprises and he didn't seem at all challenged by his sidemen as he had been with Trane and Adderley.

His protégé, John Coltrane, was becoming the most revolutionary player of this time and probably of the entire history of African-American music. Trane's music continued to change, and his solid leadership was an oasis to the younger, struggling musicians. These two took opposite directions, but Miles's forte was hard bop, where he operated most consistently; and naturally he would not move quickly into a form vanguarded by players for whom he had so much negative criticism in the past. His style of playing short phrases, now both melodic and rhythmic in their interest, was not really bursting; although recently he had shown a consistent preference for power bursts, strong statements which scream out of the horn, something that Coltrane preferred building up to and sustaining for long periods of time. Miles's burst might be on one note but would never be sustained. In the middle sixties when he began to really improvise longer, he would build statements which would climax in the middle of the improvisation instead of the middle of each chorus, as he had done earlier. Considering how long he had to struggle to acquire the great maneuverability he had, it is understandable that he was determined to protect his niche and deal with it for a while. He was still playing the very best music in the hard bop tradition; he knew this and understood what it meant to him artistically and financially.

His style had evolved, above all, into a tremendous proficiency in the area where he heard music. He used the upper part of the horn to underline a point, to make that point profound. Sometimes it was a rhythmic phrase which came from the line of the material. In the dramatic way he played, this material becomes clearly articulated in the upper part of the horn and always at the perfect point in the improvisation. Of the many ballads he had now specialized on, none used his

remarkable inventiveness as much as "Stella by Starlight" and "My Funny Valentine." He had used the
latter in his repertoire as far back as 1955, so by the
time he played it in 1964 at a benefit for CORE in
Philharmonic Hall in New York, it had become one of
his masterpieces. The piece (see transcription) is begun
in a melancholy manner by pianist Herbie Hancock.
Then Miles enters, playing the very beginning fragment and repeating it; then, beginning low in the horn,
suddenly he twists four notes of this fragment into a
two-octave sequential figure, increasing the dynamics.
He holds his listeners' interest by playing every note
as if it were the most important note he would ever
play. It is this intensity that is so persuasive in his playing, this involved melodic style that captures the experience right off the bat, as if he had been playing
for twenty minutes although he has only begun. After
this introduction, he is ready to start in earnest and
immediately takes the piece out of its starting key. And
if Ron Carter wasn't the irrepressible bassist that he
is, the piece might have gotten away from him. What
Miles plays from here on in is only vaguely similar to
the original melody, but one can hear the movement
of the piece if one listens to the progressions. The piece
changes tempo several times and, at the end, double-
times, with Miles relating to everything like a duck
relates to water. He is clearly in command. Moving in
that stunted way of his continually puts everyone off
balance except himself and the other members of the
band. Where it once had been an indication of his
groping, now it became a part of his total style which
he exploited when he felt it necessary. His dialoguing
continues in this piece, but now the sentences are much
longer and more intricate. He has learned how to use

the chromatic scale very effectively and can control his
horn so well and has such great use of the lower
register, the part of the horn which most trumpeters
avoid, that when he plays the highest note in his solo
($E^{b'''}$), it sounds as if it is a million miles away from
the lowest note he has played (A^b). It was over two
octaves and a perfect fifth. Miles makes quick musical
decisions now, because his preparation enables him to
change his mind in the middle of a phrase and still
execute it perfectly. He can bend notes to their quarter
tones just by the use of the valve. And on "Valentine,"
he prepares for the highest note by playing a two-note
phrase three times, which spans an octave just a half-
step below the highest note. In spite of this progress,
there was a strong feeling of nostalgia in the music he
played in this concert. He played twelve pieces, which
was unusually high, but of those, nine were pieces he
had been playing since the fifties, so everything was
pretty predictable. He should have been able to deal
expertly with the music. Except for the ballads, he was
also playing these pieces at a much quicker pace and
there were still some times when he seemed to be muttering lines rather than articulating them. His rhythmic
phrasing was now just incredible, in the way he could
change or begin a pattern with bits of another pattern,
or in the way he would start a pattern obviously going
to another line but stop, completely change direction,
and still be right where he wanted to be. One of the
reasons he muttered so much is that he was playing
lines that would move two ways chromatically or move
in the higher voice chromatically, holding a root; and
he played now at a much faster tempo than when he
had serious technical problems ten years before.

One of the little-known facts, but one that is

highly significant in understanding Miles's total musical self, is that between George Coleman's departure and Wayne Shorter's arrival, multi-instrumentalist Sam Rivers played in the band; in fact, he was with them for a little over six months. Along with the band, Rivers accompanied Miles on his only trip to Japan, playing all over that country. They made a tape there which has never been released in this country. On that tape, Rivers plays as strongly as anyone Miles had had in the band since John Coltrane. It is hindsight now to speculate about what might have evolved from a longer relationship between these two, but without question Rivers is one of the strongest voices out there today, both as an instrumentalist and as a composer. It probably came as a surprise to him that Miles discontinued his tenure in the band after six months and replaced him with Shorter. Listening to this one available tape with Rivers in the Miles Davis band, it becomes apparent that his contribution was considerable. Considering how far he has grown in comparison to Shorter in the ensuing years, so much that it cannot be measured, perhaps this decision to replace Rivers was significant to Miles's own musical growth.

The music that came out of the band that included Wayne Shorter, Tony Williams, Ron Carter, and Herbie Hancock was, for the first time, moving toward being a little less constricted by harmonics, although the music they performed publicly was still influenced by Miles's fifties period. The new written music, "E.S.P.," "R.J.," "Eighty-one," "Little One," "The Sorcerer," "Madness," "Hand Jive," and "Mood," is all written either by Miles or by other members of this outfit. All were executed expertly and had brief lines, lines that could be moved away from quickly. On "E.S.P.," Miles is particularly comfortable. The tempo is up, and Miles plays three climactic, developing episodes, with speed and articulation rarely heard from him before. The piece itself is sixteen bars long, eight and then a repeat, and, as always, his symmetry is really something to admire. His first climactic statement is a four-note phrase at the end of the first chorus (he takes six). By climactic statement I mean his obvious movement into the higher register. The next comes at the beginning of the fourth chorus and is also a four-note phrase. And the third, at the beginning of the final chorus, is a rocket shot, quickly slipping chromatically down, then back up again. His conservation is still in short subdivisions, because that is where he works best, and remains primarily in the center of the horn. Miles, with his technique now cleaned up, is irrepressible, his music taking a decided step toward liberation.

Miles's confidence in the new music he was producing must have been somewhat shaky because his public appearances still included "Stella by Starlight" and "All Blues," music which was new at one time but was now warmed over for the people. It was no longer a problem with his musicianship but his taste. Even some of the new music had that melancholy feeling to it, although it was apparent that this band could literally play anything it wanted to play. The piece, "Circle," (See transcription) which was taped on October 24, 1966, is a beautiful composition which Miles played meticulously and planned painstakingly; but he had been doing that for years, so it was hard to believe that this was any different from the classic medium- and slow-tempo pieces which first made him famous in the middle fifties. Pieces like "Circle" have a tendency to date Miles and, rightly, to betray that he had become comfortable; unquestionably, Miles was settling in. As complex as this new written music was harmonically, it still wasn't very innovative to be lingering in a system that Miles must have understood to be defunct.

One of the pitfalls of success is that musical development often stops if one becomes convinced that he has reached the point where his genius lies. What this complacency really says is that one is not willing to grow. Being an art form, music must always continue to move and grow, taking on the assets, throwing off the liabilities. Miles has continued to grow, but most of that growth has been to compensate for his deficiencies on the trumpet. So he learned to play faster with a greater range facility, but he was playing the things he had always played, only faster or higher. His music was becoming predictable; he would exploit the higher part of his horn but not play anything sustained in that area. He rarely ventured out of the harmonic center, which really seems a pity, because Miles can play, proving it as early as 1955, music that doesn't follow progressions. But actually, on those takes where he moved away from the progressions, he is said to have been arrogant and defiant, since they were unauthorized sessions. On "Riot," recorded June 22, 1967, there isn't any harmonic movement, but Miles and Carter play an absolutely stunning polyphonic free improvisation in which Miles demonstrates exactly what he can do; he occasionally looks to Carter for direction, but that is what collective improvisation is all about. Certainly in the same category as Chambers and Heath, Carter stays on the pulse almost all the way, with an occasional skip. The tempo is up (M.M. $\downarrow$ = 200), at a pulse which Miles only recently learned to negotiate with ease. He roams into the last chorus on all pistons, while Carter begins to play a line that is moving in a five-note pattern, playing F-E-E^b down to B^b, then to B; Carter repeats this pattern eight times, transposing it up a half-step, then down a step. In preparation for this pattern, Carter preceded it with a transposing pattern, much like this, all through the bass but never repeating it. Meanwhile Miles plays about four different rhythmic patterns, all totally different. After Carter plays his fourth repeated pattern, Miles takes a quarter-note rest, reentering just before Carter begins to transpose. The improvisation ends with Miles playing Carter's figure. Besides many other outstanding gifts, Carter plays stronger higher on the strings (near the bridge) than most bass players around. This is just one of the many interesting things that Miles and Carter do. In approximately the middle of Miles's improvisation, he and Carter dance together, beginning at measure 83 (ca.), with Carter doing a beautiful skipping syncopation which, by the way, he executes with unbelievable grace, and with Miles playing a dancing staccato around Carter's syncopation. They meet with the sensitivity that two artists of their magnitude would be expected to manifest. Carter does short glissandos which slightly vary what he is doing most of the time on the pulse; they show their potential clearly in the mutuality of the effort.

On this same day, they also recorded "Hand Jive," written by Tony Williams, which is at a little slower tempo (M.M. ♩ =184), from the same mold as "Riot," but with Williams much more dominating, stimulating Miles and Carter to play more aggressively. Miles still has his quirks. Sometimes he sounds as if he is playing on a horn overflowing with saliva, but he is so rhythmically creative that it just becomes part of his style. Although his music is tight, here he shows that it is elastic enough to move out of being redundant. It is really testimony to his own maturation, movement, and great confidence in his own ability. But the other pieces on this session, written pieces, are not nearly as inventive, remaining dependent upon centers of either major or minor scales, or one of the modes. This newer music was not the music he was playing in public; the band's concert engagements were still Miles Davis' 1950's hits, played in a different way, creative but anywhere from seven to ten years old. Wayne Shorter seems uncomfortable on the more liberated music and, on the two pieces mentioned above, stays very close to the melody line. Hancock has brilliant linearity and is consistently playing interesting rhythms but his playing seems to have too strong a structure.

When Miles gets an idea, it takes him a long time to reach the stage where it comes out all at once. The four dates that make up *Filles de Kilimanjaro* just whet one's appetite, slightly exposing the potential of the band. Miles was never as potent as he was on "Petits Machins (Little Stuff)."[21] He ranges two octaves and a minor third, playing consistently high phrases over longer periods of time. He doesn't use the lower range of the trumpet, but this is still a very bright solo, bursting with more control, articulating clearly. He is really doing new things, things which haven't been documented before. It is not one of his longer solos. "Madness" exceeds it in length, but on it, in his condensed way of dealing with music, he enters, plays, and leaves. He skillfully uses one three-note motif, which first appears in measure 2 of his improvisation and then shows up, in some form, twenty-seven times over the one hundred and nine measures he plays. He had never played anything quite like the series of

21 A transcription by David Baker can be found in *Down Beat*, December 25, 1969, pp. 44 and 47.

triplets he plays between measures 94 and 98, and certainly not beginning as high as he does (F‴). His use of triplets makes a traceable evolution throughout his career; his use of the chromatic scale for runs is another one of his patented devices. This is a fully matured Miles Davis moving at will. This is the Miles of whom we had a hint when he first began to record. His potential finally becomes realized in this absolutely brilliant solo. However, the other solos on the four dates are not as exciting. "Frelon Brun (Brown Hornet)" has brief moments, but it is just too short to warrant any kind of substantial appraisal. His playing on the other pieces is not really too different, although his accompaniment is very strong. Shorter is very commonplace, and in comparison to the other tenor players around at the time, there is not much happening with him. Miles has always played more strongly and forcefully with a strong sideman; Shorter's overall weakness failed this and forced his own musical personality to become completely subordinated by Miles's.

The music in the band had become very episodic, consisting of long written parts which often preempted improvisation, at least in importance. In 1969 on "In a Silent Way" (see transcription) the piece moves beautifully and Miles's playing far outshadows Shorter, who is playing soprano sax with a very weak sound. It seems that Miles was definitely liberating himself from the harmonic centers of the European tradition. He wasn't doing anything more inventive than what he did on "Petits Machins," but his solos were longer. Somehow the path the music takes through a labyrinth of events produces nothing that can be considered up-tempo, and the sound is sterile. The three pianos are very linear. The potential in using three pianos concentrating on rhythms is infinite, but here rhythms and any sustained rhythmic figures are practically nonexistent, except in elementary forms. The pianists play beautiful streams of lines, but the tradition of this music lies in Africa, and that means the piano should be played percussively, like its predecessor, the sanza (thumb-piano). The inactivity of the music, with Miles really sustaining the whole thing but not playing too long, although longer than usual, indicated some problems. Some would say that part of the problem was that Miles was using too many white players; this may be true in terms of economics, because there were so many brothers who could have played at least as well as the white players on these dates. It seems strange that they weren't given the gig because Miles certainly had his choice of personnel, and he could have given the money to brothers who needed it.

In spite of that fact, the music in the band was at least moving, Miles was the force, and his musicianship was finally equal to his musical ideas. He seemed to be coming to grips with another commitment, this time, to harmonically liberated music. His music in public was still not exactly like that, but he was willing to document this new commitment. He was still in his old repertoire. Incidentally, his latest records were selling at an all-time low, and suddenly he was faced with a problem of sink or swim. The result was *Bitches Brew*. Along with the obvious chauvinistic implications of the title, there is an implicit admission that the music is not happening at all. Miles is overtly using technology for its own sake, hardly playing at all; what he is playing is a phrase here and there, a burst up the chromatic scale, or a blasting little phrase in the high register. Even the facts of life have to be explained to Miles Davis; that is, white promoters will never pay for

African-American culture unless it sells. So one must either self-produce or change his music. Miles changed his music.

The band on *Bitches Brew* has incredible talent; they are Garry Bartz, soprano sax, Jack DeJohnette, drums, Keith Jarrett, keyboard, and, in the interim, Stuart Grossman, sax (shades of Dave Schildkraut!). One only has to go back to "In a Silent Way," and note what Miles was doing there, in order to realize that he has stepped backward on *Bitches Brew* and its lineage. But even on the earlier dates, there was an indication that something really wrong was happening. Those dates were very sluggish and monotonous, and Miles's playing, though the strongest on the dates, is greatly outlogged by the rhythm section when it comes to improvisation time. It seems that Miles's solo will never come, and when it does, he plays the same thing as before with nowhere near the spark of "Petits Machins." There really seems to be nothing happening at all, like the longest airplane ever made going down the longest runway ever built and never getting off the ground. There is a strong stationary feeling to the music as well as to Miles's playing; it's as if he had given up.

The only piece on the collection of *Bitches Brew* which hints of any strength coming from Miles is "Sanctuary" (see Appendix), but, as stunning as it is, it is only a repeated statement. The music since then has been just other variations of this new theme. Miles plays very little, using as many aids as possible, taking advantage of rhythm actually to cover his sometimes very sad solos, and culminating in "On the Corner," which is an insult to the intellect of the people. But there really is no sense in moralizing or making value judgments about all this activity. Miles Davis makes

music, and he has the right to make money. And the
people have the right to criticize.
    I said earlier that Miles was a revolutionary musi-
cian. Looking at his total contribution to the music of
African-American people, one sees he unquestionably
is. He demonstrated a different way to play trumpet,
and he adapted the instrument to accommodate where
he heard music. He revived interest in the mute, and
the intensity of his sound changed the tonal character
of the instrument into a completely stylized version.
His rhythmic style was the most intimate, intricate
dialogue of its time, although it caused him to be
short-lived as an improviser. The key to his style was
continually playing rhythmic phrases in continually
changing patterns with constant accent movement, all
very well-connected. When Trane began to play longer
and longer solos, Miles, with his compact style, found
it difficult to move. Miles also provided a forum for
the most revolutionary player of our time, John Coltrane, and a rhythm section that permitted Trane really
to deal; Paul Chambers was the most complete bassist
of his time, and Philly Joe Jones was one of the first
new drummers to introduce multidirectional patterns.
Cannonball Adderley just blossomed in the band and
contributed immensely to this revolutionary sextet.
Miles popularized the flügelhorn, and his interpretation
of ballads stands as a landmark for the trumpet before
or since. He influenced every trumpet player of his
time, and his bands are admired and emulated by
many other musicians. His work for orchestra was also
stunning and completely accommodated his style. He
was one of the uncompromising musicians of his time,
greatly inspiring me as a young man growing up, as
his music has done for countless admirers and students
of our music.

RECORDING SESSIONS

The following is a listing of the recording sessions in which Miles Davis played. I have omitted the names of the record albums since I am primarily concerned with the dates and personnel involved, and because there is such confusion over issues. (For a discography, including titles and labels and broadcast dates as well, I recommend that compiled by Jorgen Grunnet Jepsen and published by Karl Emil Knudsen, Denmark, 1969.) On the personnel listings, the names with one star are the leaders of those specific sessions. In the cases where various personnel replacements were used on individual takes, I have included all the players involved in one group. The pieces with two stars are Miles Davis' own compositions.

DATE & PLACE	PIECES	PERSONNEL
May 4, 1945 New York	That's the Stuff You Gonna Watch Pointless Mama Blues Deep Sea Blues Bring It on Home	Miles Davis (trumpet) *Herbie Fields (alto & tenor sax) Johnny Mehegan (piano) Al Casey (guitar) Slam Stewart (bass) Lionel Hampton (drums) Rubberlegs Williams (vocals)
May 6, 1945 New York	Just Relaxin' Run Down Camp Meeting Four O'clock Blues	Miles Davis (trumpet) *Herbie Fields (clarinet & tenor sax) Arnett Cobb (tenor sax) Lionel Hampton (piano) Al Casey (guitar) Slam Stewart (bass) Fred Radcliffe (drums)
November 26, 1945 New York	Billie's Bounce (5 takes) Now's the Time (4 takes) Thriving on a Riff (3 takes)	Miles Davis (trumpet) *Charlie Parker (alto sax) Dizzy Gillespie (piano) Argonne Thornton (piano) Curley Russell (bass) Max Roach (drums)
March 28, 1946 Los Angeles	Moose and Mooch (2 takes) Yardbird Suite (2 takes) Ornithology (3 takes) Famous Alto Break Night in Tunisia (2 takes)	Miles Davis (trumpet) *Charlie Parker (alto sax) Lucky Thompson (tenor sax) Dodo Marmarosa (piano) Arv Garrison (guitar) Victor McMillan (bass) Roy Porter (drums)
Late spring, 1946 Los Angeles	He's Gone The Story of Love	Miles Davis } Vern Carlson } trumpet Henry Coker (trombone) Boots Musulli (alto sax) Lucky Thompson (tenor sax)

ATE & PLACE	PIECES	PERSONNEL
		Herb Carol (baritone sax) Buddy Colette (tenor sax, flute) Buzz Wheeler (piano) *Charlie Mingus (bass, cello) Warren Thompson (drums) Herb Gayle (vocals)
ptember 6, 1946 os Angeles	Oo Bop Sh'Bam I Love the Loveliness In the Still of the Night Jelly Jelly	Miles Davis } Hobart Dotson } trumpet Leonard Hawkins } King Kolax } Walter Knox } Chips Outcalt } trombone Gerald Valentine } Sonny Stitt } alto sax John Cobbs } Gene Ammons } tenor sax Arthur Samsons } Cecil Payne (baritone sax) Linton Garner (piano) Connie Wainright (guitar) Tommy Potter (bass) Art Blakey (drums) *Billy Eckstine (vocals)
ctober 10, 1946 os Angeles	My Silent Love Time on My Hands All the Things You Are In a Sentimental Mood	Same personnel as above, strings added
arly 1947 ew York	All of Me Blues for Sale What's New Serenade in Blue Solitude Sophisticated Lady	Miles Davis } Hobart Dotson } trumpet Leonard Hawkins } Doug Mettome } Earl Hardy } Chippy Outcalt } trombone Gerald Valentine }

DATE & PLACE	PIECES	PERSONNEL
		*Billy Eckstine (trombone, vocals)
		Clap Dungee ⎱ alto sax
		Norris Turney ⎰
		Gene Ammons ⎱ tenor sax
		Frank Wess ⎰
		Martin Kelly (baritone sax)
		Linton Garner (piano)
		Connie Wainright (guitar)
		Bill McMahon (bass)
		Art Blakey (drums)
		strings
March 1947 New York	For Europeans Only Big Dog You Left Me Alone Jivin' with Jack the Bellboy	Miles Davis ⎱ Joe Newman ⎰ trumpet Marion Hazel Fats Navarro
		Gus Cappel ⎱ Fred Robinson ⎰ trombone Ted Kelly Dicky Wells
		Ray Perry ⎱ alto sax Jimmy Powell ⎰
		George Nicholas ⎱ tenor sa: *Illinois Jacquet ⎰
		Bill Doggett/Leonard Feath (piano)
		Al Lucas (bass)
		Shadow Wilson (drums)
May 1947 New York	**Donna Lee (4 takes) Chasin' the Bird (3 takes) Cheryl (2 takes) Buzzy (5 takes)	Miles Davis (trumpet) *Charlie Parker (alto sax) Bud Powell (piano) Tommy Potter (bass) Max Roach (drums)
August 1947 New York	**Milestones (2 takes) Little Willie Leaps (3 takes)	*Miles Davis (trumpet) *Charlie Parker (alto sax) John Lewis (piano)

DATE & PLACE	PIECES	PERSONNEL
	Wailing Willie Half Nelson (2 takes) Sippin' at Bells (3 takes)	Nelson Boyd (bass) Max Roach (drums)
October 28, 1947 New York	Dexterity (2 takes) Bongo Bop (2 takes) Prezology Dewey Square (2 takes) The Hymn Superman Bird of Paradise (2 takes) Embraceable You (2 takes)	Miles Davis (trumpet) *Charlie Parker (alto sax) Duke Jordan (piano) Tommy Potter (bass) Max Roach (drums)
November 4, 1947 New York	Bird Feathers Klactoveedstene (2 takes) Scrapple from the Apple My Old Flame Out of Nowhere Don't Blame Me	Same personnel as above
December 17, 1947 New York	Drifting on a Reed (3 takes) Quasimodo (2 takes) Charlie's Wig (2 takes) Bongo Bop Bird Feathers (2 takes) Crazeology (4 takes) How Deep Is the Ocean (2 takes)	Miles Davis (trumpet) J. J. Johnson (trombone) *Charlie Parker (alto sax) Duke Jordan (piano) Tommy Potter (bass) Max Roach (drums)

DATE & PLACE	PIECES	PERSONNEL
Late 1947 New York	Bean-A-Re-Bop Phantomesque The Way You Look Tonight Isn't It Romantic	Miles Davis (trumpet) Kai Winding (trombone) Howard Johnson (alto sax) *Coleman Hawkins (tenor sax) Hank Jones (piano) Tommy Potter (bass) Max Roach (drums)

Late December
1947
Detroit
	Another Hair-Do
	    (3 takes)
	Blue Bird (2 takes)
	Klaunstance
	Bird Gets the Worm
	    (2 takes)
		Miles Davis (trumpet)
		*Charlie Parker (alto sax)
		Duke Jordan (piano)
		Tommy Potter (bass)
		Max Roach (drums)

Spring 1948
New York
(broadcast)
	52nd Street Theme
	    (3 takes)
	Shaw' Nuff
	Hot House
	Out of Nowhere
	    (2 takes)
	This Time the
	    Dream's on Me
	    (2 takes)
	A Night in Tunisia
	How High the Moon
	Dizzy Atmosphere
	The Way You Look
	    Tonight
	Chasin' the Bird
	My Old Flame
		Same personnel as above

August 29, 1948 New York	Barbados (4 takes) Ah-Leu-Cha (2 takes) Constellation (4 takes)	Miles Davis (trumpet) *Charlie Parker (alto sax) John Lewis (piano) Curley Russell (bass) Max Roach (drums)

ATE & PLACE	PIECES	PERSONNEL
ugust– ptember, 1948 ew York	Perhaps (6 takes) Marmaduke (6 takes) Steeplechase Merry-Go-Round (2 takes)	Same personnel as above
ptember 4, 1948 ew York roadcast)	Ko-Ko 52nd Street Theme	Miles Davis (trumpet) °Charlie Parker (alto sax) Tadd Dameron (piano) Curley Russell (bass) Max Roach (drums)
ecember 11, 1948 ew York roadcast)	Big Foot Groovin' High Ornithology	Miles Davis (trumpet) °Charlie Parker (alto sax) Al Haig (piano) Tommy Potter (bass) Max Roach (drums)
ecember 12, 1948 ew York roadcast)	Hot House Salt Peanuts	Same personnel as above
cember 18, 1948 ew York roadcast)	Out of Nowhere How High the Moon	Same personnel as above
nuary 3, 1949 ew York	Overtime (2 takes) Victory Ball	Metronome All Stars: Fats Navarro ⎫ Miles Davis ⎬ trumpet Dizzy Gillespie ⎭ J. J. Johnson ⎫ trombone Kai Winding ⎭ Buddy DeFranco (clarinet) Charlie Parker (alto sax) Charlie Ventura (tenor sax) Ernie Gaceras (baritone sax) Lennie Tristano (piano) Billy Bauer (guitar)

DATE & PLACE	PIECES	PERSONNEL
		Eddie Safranski (bass) Shelly Manne (drums)
January 21, 1949 New York	Jeru Move Godchild **Budo	*Miles Davis (trumpet) Kai Winding (trombone) Junior Collins (French hor) Bill Barber (tuba) Lee Konitz (alto sax) Gerry Mulligan (baritone sa) Al Haig (piano) Joe Shulman (bass) Max Roach (drums)
April 21, 1949 New York	John's Delight Focus	Miles Davis (trumpet) J. J. Johnson (trombone) Ed Gregory (alto sax) Benjamin Lundy (tenor sax) Cecil Payne (baritone sax) *Tadd Dameron (piano) John Collins (guitar) Curley Russell (bass) Kenny Clarke (drums)
April 22, 1949 New York	Venus de Milo Rouge Boplicity Israel	*Miles Davis (trumpet) J. J. Johnson (trombone) Sandy Siegelstein (French horn) Bill Barber (tuba) Lee Konitz (alto sax) Gerry Mulligan (baritone sa) John Lewis (piano) Nelson Boyd (bass) Kenny Clarke (drums)
March 9, 1950	**Deception Rocker Moon Dreams Darn That Dream	*Miles Davis (trumpet) J. J. Johnson (trombone) Gunther Schuller (French horn)

DATE & PLACE	PIECES	PERSONNEL
		Bill Barber (tuba) Lee Konitz (alto sax) Gerry Mulligan (baritone sax) John Lewis (piano) Al McKibbon (bass) Max Roach (drums) Kenny Hagood (vocals)
May 18, 1950 New York	Ain't Misbehavin' Goodnight My Love It Might As Well Be Spring	Miles Davis (trumpet) Benny Green (trombone) Tony Scott (clarinet) Bud Johnson (tenor sax) °Jimmy Jones (piano) Freddie Green (guitar) Billy Taylor (bass) Mundell Lowe (guitar) J. C. Heard (drums) °Sarah Vaughan (vocals)
May 19, 1950 New York	Mean to Me	Same personnel as above
January 17, 1951 New York	Au Privave (2 takes) She Rote (2 takes) K. C. Blues Star Eyes	Miles Davis (trumpet) °Charlie Parker (alto sax) Walter Bishop (piano) Teddy Kotick (bass) Max Roach (drums)
January 17, 1951 New York	Morpheus °°Down Blue Room (2 takes) Whispering	°Miles Davis (trumpet, piano) Benny Green (trombone) Sonny Rollins (tenor sax) John Lewis (piano) Percy Heath (bass) Roy Haynes (drums)
January 17, 1951 New York	I Know	°Sonny Rollins (tenor sax) Miles Davis (piano)

DATE & PLACE	PIECES	PERSONNEL
		Percy Heath (bass) Roy Haynes (drums)
January 24, 1951 New York	Early Spring	Metronome All Stars: Miles Davis (trumpet) Kai Winding (trombone) John LaPorta (clarinet) Lee Konitz (alto sax) Stan Getz (tenor sax) Serge Chaloff (baritone sax) Terry Gibbs (vibes) George Shearing (piano) Billy Bauer (guitar) Eddie Safranski (bass) Max Roach (drums)
March 8, 1951 New York	Odjenar Ezz-Thetic Hi-Beck Yesterdays	Miles Davis (trumpet) *Lee Konitz (alto sax) Sal Mosca (piano) Billy Bauer (guitar) Arnold Fishkin (bass) Max Roach (drums)
October 5, 1951 New York	Conception **Out of the Blue **Denial **Bluing Dig My Old Flame Paper Moon	*Miles Davis (trumpet) Jackie McLean (alto sax) Sonny Rollins (tenor sax) Walter Bishop (piano) Tommy Potter (bass) Art Blakey (drums)
May 9, 1952 New York	Dear Old Stockholm Chance It Donna (2 takes) Woody'n You (2 takes) Yesterdays How Deep Is the Ocean	*Miles Davis (trumpet) J. J. Johnson (trombone) Jackie McLean (alto sax) Gil Goggins (piano) Oscar Pettiford (bass) Kenny Clarke (drums)

DATE & PLACE	PIECES	PERSONNEL
January 30, 1953 New York	Compulsion The Serpent's Tooth (2 takes) 'Round Midnight	°Miles Davis (trumpet) Sonny Rollins (tenor sax) Charlie "Chan" Parker (tenor sax) Walter Bishop (piano) Percy Heath (bass) Philly Joe Jones (drums)
February 19, 1953 New York	Tasty Pudding Willie the Weeper Floppy For Adults Only	°Miles Davis (trumpet) Sonny Truitt (trombone) Al Cohn ⎱ tenor sax Zoot Sims ⎰ John Lewis (piano) Leonard Gaskin (bass) Kenny Clarke (drums)
April 20, 1953 New York	Tempus Fugit (2 takes) Enigma Ray's Idea (2 takes) I Waited for You Kelo C.T.A. (2 takes)	°Miles Davis (trumpet) J. J. Johnson (trombone) Jimmy Heath (tenor sax) Gil Goggins (piano) Percy Heath (bass) Art Blakey (drums)
May 19, 1953 New York	When Lights Are Low Tune Up °°Miles Ahead °°Smooch	°Miles Davis (trumpet) John Lewis (piano) Charlie Mingus (piano) Percy Heath (bass) Max Roach (drums)
March 6, 1954 New York	°°Lazy Susan It Never Entered My Mind °°Weirdo °°Take-Off °°The Leap Well You Needn't	°Miles Davis (trumpet) Horace Silver (piano) Percy Heath (bass) Art Blakey (drums)

DATE & PLACE	PIECES	PERSONNEL
March 15, 1954 New York	**Blue Haze Four That Old Devil Called Love	*Miles Davis (trumpet) Horace Silver (piano) Percy Heath (bass) Art Blakey (drums)
April 3, 1954 New York	Love Me or Leave Me I'll Remember April **Solar You Don't Know What Love Is	*Miles Davis (trumpet) Dave Schildkraut (alto sax) Horace Silver (piano) Percy Heath (bass) Kenny Clarke (drums)
April 29, 1954 New York	Walkin' Blue 'n' Boogie	*Miles Davis (trumpet) J. J. Johnson (trombone) Lucky Thompson (tenor sax Horace Silver (piano) Percy Heath (bass) Kenny Clarke (drums)
June 29, 1954 New York	But Not for Me (2 takes) Doxy Oleo Airegin	*Miles Davis (trumpet) Sonny Rollins (tenor sax) Horace Silver (piano) Percy Heath (bass) Kenny Clarke (drums)
December 24, 1954 New York	**Swing Spring The Man I Love (2 takes) Bags' Groove (2 takes) Bemsha Swing	*Miles Davis (trumpet) Thelonious Monk (piano) Milt Jackson (vibes) Percy Heath (bass) Kenny Clarke (drums)
June 7, 1955 New York	A Night in Tunisia I See Your Face Before Me **I Didn't A Gal in Calico **Green Haze Will You Still Be Mine?	*Miles Davis (trumpet) Red Garland (piano) Oscar Pettiford (bass) Philly Joe Jones (drums)

DATE & PLACE	PIECES	PERSONNEL
July 9, 1955 New York	Easy Living Alone Together Nature Boy There Is No You	°Miles Davis (trumpet) Britt Woodman (trombone) Teddy Charles (vibes) Charles Mingus (bass) Elvin Jones (drums)
August 5, 1955 New York	Minor March Blues Changes Dr. Jekyll Bitty Ditty	°Miles Davis (trumpet) Jackie McLean (alto sax) Milt Jackson (vibes) Ray Bryant (piano) Percy Heath (bass) Art Taylor (drums)
October 27, 1955 New York	°°Budo Ah-Leu-Cha	°Miles Davis (trumpet) John Coltrane (tenor sax) Red Garland (piano) Paul Chambers (bass) Philly Joe Jones (drums)
November 16, 1955 New York	°°Miles' Theme How Am I to Know? S'posin' Stablemates Just Squeeze Me There Is No Greater Love	Same personnel as above
March 16, 1956 New York	°°No Line In Your Own Sweet Way °°Weird Blues	°Miles Davis (trumpet) Sonny Rollins (tenor sax) Tommy Flanagan (piano) Paul Chambers (bass) Art Taylor (drums)
May 11, 1956 New York	Diane Salt Peanuts °°The Theme, I °°The Theme, II	°Miles Davis (trumpet) John Coltrane (tenor sax) Red Garland (piano) Paul Chambers (bass)

DATE & PLACE	PIECES	PERSONNEL
	It Never Entered My Mind Trane's Blues In Your Own Sweet Way The Surrey with the Fringe On Top Four Woody'n You When I Fall In Love Something I Dreamed Last Night It Could Happen to You	Philly Joe Jones (drums)
June 5, 1956 New York	Tadd's Delight Dear Old Stockholm Bye Bye Blackbird	Same personnel as above
September 10, 1956 New York	Sweet Sue All of You 'Round Midnight	*Miles Davis (trumpet) John Coltrane (tenor sax) Red Garland (piano) Paul Chambers (bass) Philly Joe Jones (drums)
October 20, 1956 New York	Three Little Feelings	Miles Davis (trumpet, flügelhorn) Melvyn Broiles ⎫ Carmine Fornatotto ⎪ Bernie Glow ⎬ trumpe[t] John Ware ⎪ Art Slatter ⎪ Joe Wilder ⎭ Urbie Green ⎫ J. J. Johnson ⎬ trombone John Clark ⎭

DATE & PLACE	PIECES	PERSONNEL
		Joe Singer ⎫
		Jim Buffington ⎬ French horn
		Art Sussman ⎪
		Ray Alonge ⎭
		Bill Barber (tuba)
		John Swallow ⎱ baritone horn
		Ron Richette ⎰
		Milt Hinton (bass)
		Osie Johnson (drums)
		Richard Harowitz (percussion)
October 23, 1956 New York	Poem for Brass	Same personnel as above
October 26, 1956 New York	Oleo My Funny Valentine 'Round Midnight If I Were a Bell ** Blues by Five You're My Everything Well You Needn't Half Nelson When Lights Are Low Tune Up I Could Write a Book Airegin	* Miles Davis (trumpet) John Coltrane (tenor sax) Red Garland (piano) Paul Chambers (bass) Philly Joe Jones (drums)
May 6, 1957 New York	The Duke The Maids of Cadiz	* Miles Davis (flügelhorn) Taft Jordan ⎫ Louis Mucci ⎪ John Carisi ⎬ trumpet Bernie Glow ⎪ Ernie Royal ⎭ Joe Bennett ⎫ Frank Rehak ⎬ trombone Jimmy Cleveland ⎭

DATE & PLACE	PIECES	PERSONNEL
		Tom Mitchell (bass trombone Jim Buffington ⎫ Willie Ruff ⎬ French horn Tony Miranda ⎭ Bill Barber (tuba) Lee Konitz (alto sax) Danny Bank (bass clarinet) Sid Cooper ⎫ Romeo Penque ⎬ flute, clarine Edwin Laine ⎭ Paul Chambers (bass) Art Taylor (drums) °Gil Evans (conductor, arranger)
May 10, 1957 New York	°°Miles Ahead My Ship	Same personnel as above
May 23, 1957 New York	Blues for Pablo New Rhumba Springsville	Same personnel as above

May 27, 1957
New York
	Lament
	I Don't Wanna Be
	  Kissed
	The Meaning of the
	  Blues
		Same personnel as above

December 4, 1957
Paris
	°°Au Bar du Petit Bac
	°°Florence sur les
	    Champs-Elysées
	°°Chez le Photographe
	    du Motel
	°°Sur l'Autoroute
	°°Julien dans
	    l'Ascenseur
	°°Generique
	°°Diner au Hotel
	°°L'Assassinat de Carala
		°Miles Davis (trumpet)
		Barney Wilen (tenor sax)
		Rene Urtreger (piano)
		Pierre Michelot (bass)
		Kenny Clarke (drums)

DATE & PLACE	PIECES	PERSONNEL
Early 1958 New York	Bahia Maria, My Own Perfidia Adios	°Michel Legrande and His Orchestra Miles Davis (trumpet)
March 9, 1958 New York	One for Daddy-O Dancing in the Dark Love for Sale Autumn Leaves Somethin' Else	Miles Davis (trumpet) °Julian Adderley (alto sax) Hank Jones (piano) Sam Jones (bass) Art Blakey (drums)
April 2, 1958 New York	Straight, No Chaser Two Bass Hit Milestones	°Miles Davis (trumpet) Julian Adderley (alto sax) John Coltrane (tenor sax) Red Garland (piano) Paul Chambers (bass) Philly Joe Jones (drums)
April 3, 1958 New York	°°Sid's Ahead Dr. Jekyll	Same personnel as above
May 26, 1958 New York	Put Your Little Foot Out Green Dolphin Street Stella by Starlight	°Miles Davis (trumpet) Julian Adderley (alto sax) John Coltrane (tenor sax) Bill Evans (piano) Paul Chambers (bass) Jimmy Cobb (drums)
June 25, 1958 New York	'Round Midnight Wild Man The Jitterbug Waltz Django	Miles Davis (trumpet) Jerome Richardson (clarinet, bass) Phil Woods (alto sax) John Coltrane (tenor sax) Herbie Mann (flute) Betty Glaman (harp) Eddie Costa (vibes) Bill Evans (piano) Paul Chambers (bass)

DATE & PLACE	PIECES	PERSONNEL
		Kenny Dennis (drums) *Michel Legrande (conductor, arranger)
July 3, 1958 Newport Jazz Festival	Straight, No Chaser Two Bass Hit Ah-Leu-Cha Fran-Dance	*Miles Davis (trumpet) Julian Adderley (alto sax) John Coltrane (tenor sax) Bill Evans (piano) Paul Chambers (bass) Jimmy Cobb (drums)
July 22, 1958 New York	My Man's Gone Now Gone Gone, Gone, Gone	*Miles Davis (trumpet, flügelhorn) Louis Mucci ⎫ Ernie Royal ⎬ trumpet John Coles Bernie Glow ⎭ Jimmy Cleveland ⎫ Joseph Bennett ⎬ trombone Dick Hixson Frank Rehak ⎭ Willie Ruff ⎫ French Julius B. Watkins ⎬ horn Gunther Schuller ⎭ Bill Barber (tuba) Julian Adderley ⎫ alto sax Danny Banks ⎬ Phil Bodner ⎫ Romeo Benque ⎬ flute Jerome Richardson ⎭ Paul Chambers (bass) Philly Joe Jones ⎫ drums Jimmy Cobb ⎬ *Gil Evans (conductor, arranger)
July 29, 1958 New York	Here Come de Honey Man	Same personnel as above

DATE & PLACE	PIECES	PERSONNEL
	Bess, You Is My Woman Now It Ain't Necessarily So Fishermen, Straw- berry and Devil Crab	
August 4, 1958	Prayer (Oh, Doctor Jesus) Where's My Bess The Buzzard Song	Same personnel as above
August 18, 1958 New York	Summertime There's a Boat That's Leaving Soon for New York I Love You, Porgy	Same personnel as above
March 2, 1959 New York	••So What ••Freddie Freeloader ••Blue in Green	•Miles Davis (trumpet) Julian Adderley (alto sax) John Coltrane (tenor sax) Wynton Kelly (piano) Bill Evans (piano) Paul Chambers (bass) Jimmy Cobb (drums)
April 22, 1959 New York	••All Blues Flamenco Sketches	•Miles Davis (trumpet) Julian Adderley (alto sax) John Coltrane (tenor sax) Bill Evans (piano) Paul Chambers (bass) Jimmy Cobb (drums)
November 20, 1959 New York	Concierto De Aranjuez	•Miles Davis (trumpet, flügelhorn) Bernie Glow ⎫ Louis Mucci ⎬ trumpet Ernie Royal ⎪ Taft Jordan ⎭

DATE & PLACE	PIECES	PERSONNEL

Dick Hixson ⎫ trombone
Frank Rehak ⎭

John Barrows ⎫
Earl Chapin ⎬ Frenc
Jimmy Buffington ⎭ horn

Jimmy McAllister (tuba)

Eddie Caine ⎫ flute
Albert Block ⎭

Harold Feldman (oboe,
    clarinet)

Danny Bank (bass clarine

Janet Putnam (harp)

Paul Chambers (bass)

Jimmy Cobb (drums)

Elvin Jones (percussion)

*Gil Evans (conductor,
    arranger)

March 10, 1960
New York   The Pan Piper

*Miles Davis (trumpet,
    flügelhorn)

Bernie Glow ⎫
John Coles ⎬ trumpet
Ernie Royal ⎪
Louis Mucci ⎭

Dick Hixson ⎫ trombone
Frank Rehak ⎭

Tony Miranda ⎫
Jimmy Buffington ⎬ Frenc
Joe Singer ⎭ horn

Bill Barber (tuba)

Jack Knitzer (bassoon)

Harold Feldman ⎫ flute
Albert Block ⎭

Romeo Penque (oboe)

Danny Bank (bass clarine

Janet Putnam (harp)

Paul Chambers (bass)

Jimmy Cobb (drums)

ATE & PLACE	PIECES	PERSONNEL
		Elvin Jones (percussion) *Gil Evans (conductor, arranger)
arch 11, 1960 ew York	Will o' the Wisp Saeta Solea	Same personnel as above
arch 22, 1960 ockholm ncert	**All Blues Walkin'	*Miles Davis (trumpet) John Coltrane (tenor sax) Wynton Kelly (piano) Paul Chambers (bass) Jimmy Cobb (drums)
tober 13, 1960 ockholm ncert	Unknown Title	*Miles Davis (trumpet) Sonny Stitt (alto sax) Wynton Kelly (piano) Paul Chambers (bass) Jimmy Cobb (drums)
arch 7, 1961 ew York	**Pfrancing **Drag-Dog	*Miles Davis (trumpet) Hank Mobley } John Coltrane } tenor sax Wynton Kelly (piano) Paul Chambers (bass) Jimmy Cobb (drums)
arch 20, 1961 ew York	Someday My Prince Will Come Old Folks	Same personnel as above
arch 21, 1961 ew York	**Teo I Thought About You	Same personnel as above
ril 14, 15, 1961 an Francisco "he Blackhawk"	Bye Bye Blackbird Love I Found You Well You Needn't	*Miles Davis (trumpet) Hank Mobley (tenor sax) Wynton Kelly (piano)

DATE & PLACE	PIECES	PERSONNEL
	**So What	Paul Chambers (bass)
	Walkin'	Jimmy Cobb (drums)
	All of You	
	**No Blues	
	**Teo	
	If I Were a Bell	
	Oleo	
	Fran-Dance	
	Bye Bye	
April 21, 1961 San Francisco "The Blackhawk"	On Green Dolphin Street	Same personnel as above
May 19, 1961 New York (Carnegie Hall)	**So What **No Blues Oleo	Same personnel as above
May 19, 1961 New York (Carnegie Hall)	**So What Spring Is Here Someday My Prince Will Come The Meaning of the Blues Lament	*Miles Davis (trumpet) Bernie Glow ⎫ Ernie Royal ⎪ John Coles ⎬ trumpet Louis Mucci ⎭ Jimmy Knepper ⎫ Dick Hixson ⎬ trombone Frank Rehak ⎭ Paul Ingraham ⎫ Julius Watkins ⎬ French h◖ Bob Swisshelm ⎭ Bill Barber (tuba) Steve Lacy (soprano sax) Jerome Richardson ⎫ Eddie Caine ⎪ Romeo Penque ⎬ reeds Bob Triscario ⎪ Danny Bank ⎭ Janet Putnam (harp) Paul Chambers (bass)

ATE & PLACE	PIECES	PERSONNEL
		Jimmy Cobb (drums) Bob Rosengarden (percussion) °Gil Evans (conductor, arranger)
ly 27, 1962 ew York	Corvocada New Rhumba Aos Pes da Cruz (Slow Samba)	Same personnel as above
ıgust 13, 1962 ɜw York	Song No. 1 Wait Till You See Her	Same personnel as above
ıgust 21, 1962	Nothing Like You Blue Christmas	°Miles Davis (trumpet) Frank Rehak (trombone) Wayne Shorter (tenor sax) Paul Chambers (bass) Jimmy Cobb (drums) William Correa (bongo) Bob Dorough (vocals)
ıgust 23, 1962 ɜw York	Devil May Care	Same personnel as above

ʋvember 6, 1962
ɜw York
	Song No. 2
	Once Upon a
	    Summertime
		°Miles Davis (trumpet)
		Ernie Royal (trumpet)
		John Barrows ⎱ French horn
		Jimmy Buffington ⎰
		Frank Rehak (trombone)
		Wayne Shorter (tenor sax)
		Janet Putnam (harp)
		Paul Chambers (bass)
		Jimmy Cobb (drums)
		Elvin Jones (percussion)
		William Correa (bongo)
		Bob Dorough (vocals)
		°Gil Evans (conductor,
		    arranger)

DATE & PLACE	PIECES	PERSONNEL

April 16, 1963
Los Angeles
	Baby Won't You
	    Please Come
	    Home
	I Fall in Love Too
	    Easily
		°Miles Davis (trumpet)
		George Coleman (tenor sa
		Victor Feldman (piano)
		Ron Carter (bass)
		Frank Butler (drums)

April 17, 1963 Los Angeles	Summer Nights	Same personnel as above
May 14, 1963 New York	Seven Steps to Heaven Joshua So Near So Far	°Miles Davis (trumpet) George Coleman (tenor sa Herbie Hancock (piano) Ron Carter (bass) Tony Williams (drums)
July 27, 1963 Antibes, France Jazz Festival	Introduction Autumn Leaves Milestones Joshua All of You Walkin'	Same personnel as above

February 12, 1964
New York
(Philharmonic
Hall)
	°°So What
	°°All Blues
	Walkin'
	My Funny Valentine
	Joshua
	Stella by Starlight
	All of You
	I Thought About You
	°°Go Go
	There Is No Greater
	    Love
	Four
	Seven Steps to
	    Heaven
		Same personnel as above

TE & PLACE	PIECES	PERSONNEL
14, 1964 yo, Japan	If I Were a Bell My Funny Valentine °°So What! Walkin' All of You	°Miles Davis (trumpet) Sam Rivers (tenor sax) Herbie Hancock (piano) Ron Carter (bass) Tony Williams (drums)
tember 25, 1964 lin ilharmonic l)	Autumn Leaves Walkin' °°Theme °°Milestones °°So What	°Miles Davis (trumpet) Wayne Shorter (tenor sax) Herbie Hancock (piano) Ron Carter (bass) Tony Williams (drums)
uary 20, 1965 s Angeles	R.J. °°E.S.P.	Same personnel as above
uary 21, 1965 Angeles	Little One °°Eighty-one	Same personnel as above
uary 22, 1965 s Angeles	°°Agitation Iris Mood	Same personnel as above
ober 24, 1966 v York	Orbits °°Circle Dolores Freedom Jazz Dance	Same personnel as above
ober 25, 1966 v York	Footprints Ginger Bread Boy	Same personnel as above
y 16, 1967 v York	Vonetta Limbo	Same personnel as above
y 17, 1967 v York	The Sorcerer Masqualero	Same personnel as above
y 24, 1967 v York	Prince of Darkness	Same personnel as above

DATE & PLACE	PIECES	PERSONNEL
June 7, 1967 New York	Nefertiti	Same personnel as above
June 22, 1967 New York	Hand Jive Madness	Same personnel as abov
July 19, 1967 New York	Pinocchio Fall Riot	Same personnel as above
January 16, 1968 New York	Paraphernalia	*Miles Davis (trumpet) Wayne Shorter (tenor s. Herbie Hancock (piano George Benson (guitar) Ron Carter (bass) Tony Williams (drums)
May 15, 1968 New York	**Country Son	*Miles Davis (trumpet) Wayne Shorter (tenor s. Herbie Hancock (piano Ron Carter (bass) Tony Williams (drums)
May 16, 1968 New York	Black Comedy	Same personnel as abov
May 17, 1968 New York	**Stuff	Same personnel as abov
June 19, 1968 New York	**Frelon Brun (Brown Hornet)	*Miles David (trumpet) Wayne Shorter (tenor s. Herbie Hancock (piano electric piano) Ron Carter (bass) Tony Williams (drums)

ATE & PLACE	PIECES	PERSONNEL
e 21, 1968 w York	**Filles de Kilimanjaro (Girls of Kilimanjaro)	Same personnel as above
tember 24, 1968 w York	**Petits Machins (Little Stuff) **Mademoiselle Mabry (Miss Mabry)	*Miles Davis (trumpet) Wayne Shorter (tenor sax) Chick Corea (piano, electric piano) Dave Holland (bass) Tony Williams (drums)
e 20, 1968 w York	**Tout de Suite	Same personnel as above
bruary 18, 1969 w York	**Shhh/Peaceful In a Silent Way **It's About Time	*Miles Davis (trumpet) Wayne Shorter (tenor sax) Herbie Hancock (electric piano) Chick Corea (electric piano) Josef Zawinul (electric piano, organ) John McLaughlin (guitar) Dave Holland (bass) Tony Williams (drums)
gust 19, 20, 21, 9 New York	**Bitches Brew **Spanish Key **Pharaoh's Dance Sanctuary **Miles Runs the Voodoo Down **John McLaughlin	*Miles Davis (trumpet) Wayne Shorter (soprano sax) Bennie Maupin (bass clarinet) Chick Corea ⎫ Joe Zawinul ⎬ electric piano Larry Young ⎭ John McLaughlin (electric guitar) Dave Holland (bass) Harvey Brooks (Fender bass) Lenny White ⎫ Jack DeJohnette ⎬ drums Charles Alias ⎭ Jim Riley (percussion)

DATE & PLACE	PIECES	PERSONNEL
June 17, 1970 New York (Fillmore East)	**Wednesday Miles	*Miles Davis (trumpet) Steve Grossman (soprano sa⬛ Chick Corea (electric piano Keith Jarrett (organ) Dave Holland (bass) Jack DeJohnette (drums) Airto Moriera (percussion)
June 18, 1970 New York (Fillmore East)	**Thursday Miles	Same personnel as above
June 19, 1970 New York (Fillmore East)	**Friday Miles	Same personnel as above
June 20, 1970 New York (Fillmore East)	**Saturday Miles	Same personnel as above
1970 Isle of Wight/ Atlanta Pop Festival	Call It Anythin'	Miles Davis (trumpet) Personnel unknown
1970 New York	**Right Off **Yesternow	*Miles Davis (trumpet) Steve Grossman (soprano sa⬛ Herbie Hancock (keyboard John McLaughlin (guitar) Michael Henderson (bass) Jack DeJohnette (drums)
1971 (*ca.*) New York	**Little Church	*Miles Davis (trumpet) Steve Grossman (sax) Keith Jarrett ⎫ Herbie Hancock⎬ keyboard Chick Corea ⎭

TE & PLACE	PIECES	PERSONNEL
		Hermeto Pascoal (electric piano, whistling) John McLaughlin (guitar) Dave Holland (bass) Jack DeJohnette (drums) Airto Moriera (percussion)
71 (ca.) w York	**Nem Um Talvez **Selim	*Miles Davis (trumpet) Steve Grossman (soprano sax) Herbie Hancock ⎫ Keith Jarrett ⎬ keyboard Chick Corea ⎭ Ron Carter (bass) Jack DeJohnette (drums) Airto Moriera (percussion) Hermeto Pascoal (voice)
71 (ca.) ew York	**Sivad **What I Say **Funky Tonk Inamorata and Narration by Conrad Roberts	Miles Davis (trumpet) Gary Bartz (soprano sax) Keith Jarrett (piano) John McLaughlin (guitar) Michael Henderson (bass) Jack DeJohnette (drums) Airto Moriera (percussion)
971 (ca.) ew York	Medley: **Gemini Double Image	*Miles Davis (trumpet) Wayne Shorter (soprano sax) Joe Zawinul ⎫ Chick Corea ⎬ keyboard John McLaughlin (guitar) Khalil Balakrishna (sitar) Dave Holland (bass) Jack DeJohnette (drums) Airto Moriera (percussion)
une 1, 1972 New York	**On the Corner **New York Girl	*Miles Davis (trumpet) 'Carlos Garnett (tenor sax)

DATE & PLACE	PIECES	PERSONNEL
	Thinkin' One Thing and Doin' Another **Vote for Miles** **Black Satin**	Herbie Hancock ⎱ keyboar Harold J. Williams ⎰ David Creamer (guitar) Michael Henderson (bass) Colin Walcott (sitar) Badal Roy (tabla) Jack DeJohnette (drums) Bill Hart (drums) M'tume (percussion)
June 6, 1972 New York	**One and One** **Helen Butte** **Mr. Freedom X**	Same personnel as above
September 29, 1972 New York (Philharmonic Hall)	**Titles Unknown**	*Miles Davis (trumpet) Carlos Garnett (tenor sax) Cedric Lawson (organ, synthesizer) Reggie Lucas (guitar) Khalil Balakrishna (sitar) Michael Henderson (bass) Badal Roy (tabla) Al Foster (drums) M'tume (congas)

BIBLIOGRAPHY

"Aftermath for Miles." *Down Beat,* 26:11, October 29, 1959.

Albertson, Chris, "Blood, Sweat & Tears: With Miles Davis." *Down Beat* 37:18, September 17, 1970, p. 12.

——— "Unmasking of Miles Davis." *Saturday Review,* 54:67–9+, November 27, 1971.

Alessandrini, P., *et al.,* "Disques du mois" port. *Jazz Magazine,* n174:47, January 1970.

Aletti V., (Port.) "Red Roses from Laura for Miles." *Rolling Stone,* n56:20, April 16, 1970.

All Stars (Metronome). *Metronome,* 67:15, February 1951.

Anderson, J. Lee, "The Musings of Miles." *Saturday Review,* 41:58–9, October 11, 1958.

"Apollo, N.Y." *Variety,* 214:87, March 18, 1959.

Aronowitz, A., "The 11,000 dollar bash," port. *Melody Maker,* 46:24, June 5, 1971.

——— "James has the vision of a blind man," port. *Melody Maker,* 46:26, April 24, 1971.

——— "Rock is a white man's word, says Miles," port. *Melody Maker,* 45:25, October 17, 1970.

———— "Rock is a white man's word, says Miles." *Rolling Stone*, n73:54, December 24, 1970.

Arrigoni, A., "Qualcosa sta cambiando." *Musical Jazz*, 16:17–21, June, 1960.

Atterton, J., "Dave Holland at home in Harlem." *Melody Maker*, 43:8, September 7, 1968.

Austin, William W., *Music in the 20th Century*. New York: W. W. Norton, Inc., 1966.

Baker, David, "Transcription of Miles Davis' PETITS MACHINS Solo." *Down Beat*, December 25, 1969, pp. 44, 47.

Balliett, Whitney, "Chameleon" (Jazz Records). *The New Yorker*, 34:121–5, May 17, 1958.

———— "Interregnum" (Jazz Records). *The New Yorker*, 40:194–7, April 25, 1964.

———— "Musical Events—Jazz Concerts." *The New Yorker*, 37:79–80, May 27, 1961.

Berendt, Joachim E., *The New Jazz Book*, trans. Dan Morgenstern. New York: Hill and Wang, 1962.

Bianco, F., "Trionfo di Davis ad Antibes." *Musical Jazz*, 19:17–9, September 1963.

"Black Hawk, S. F." *Variety* 222:77, May 3, 1961.

Blesh, Rudi, *Shining Trumpets*. New York: Alfred A. Knopf, Inc., 1958.

"Bodyguard for Miles Davis." *Melody Maker*, 35:1, August 27, 1960.

Brown, R., "[Jack Johnson] Record reviews." *Jazz Journal*, 24:30–1, August, 1971.

Burde, W., "Jazz-Tage 1969." *Neue Zeitschrift für Musik*, 130:559, December 1970.

Burks, J., "Miles a Lot of Different Bitches." *Rolling Stone*, n62:15, July 9, 1970.

Burland, Sancha, and Reisner, Robert, "The Midnight Horn." *Nugget*, December, 1958.

Burns, J., Biog. port. "Miles Davis: The Early Years." *Jazz Journal*, 23:2–4, January 1970.

"Caught in the Act." *Down Beat*, 37:44, December 24, 1970.

"Caught in the Act," port. *Down Beat*, 37:28, July 23; port. 34, December 24, 1970.

"Caught in the Act." *Down Beat*, 28:42, July 6, 1961.

"Caught in the Act." *Down Beat*, 29:31, August 2, 1962.

"Charge Dismissed." *Down Beat*, 26:11, November 12, 1959.

Charters, Samuel B., and Kunstadt, Leonard, *Jazz—A History of the New York Scene*. New York: Doubleday & Company, Inc., 1962.

"Chronique des Disques: At Fillmore." *Jazz Hot*, n26:34, February 1971.

"Clapton & Bruce to Join Miles!" *Melody Maker*, 45:1, June 6, 1970.

Cole, W., "Caught in the Act." *Down Beat*, 38:28, April 15, 1971.

"Combo Reviews." *Variety*, 223:44, July 5, 1961.

Comment on Newport Jazz Festival notes counter NY Musician's Jazz Festival's opposition to Newport Festival and NY Musician's charge that Newport is dominated by 'white middle-class orientation'; M Davis refusal to perform at Newport Festival concert and other black musicians' disappointment with Newport arrangements discussed. *New York Times*, Jl 9, IV, 4:1, 1972. illus.

"Concert Review." *Variety*, 233:61, February 19, 1964.

"Concert Reviews." *Variety*, 263:43, August 4, 1971.

Cooke, J., "Miles Davis and Archie Shepp." *Jazz Monthly*, 13:16, December, 1967.

——— Record Review: In a Silent Way. *Jazz Monthly*, n183:19, May 1970.

Cotterrell, R., "Interlude. Miles Davis with Hank Mobley." *Jazz Monthly*, 13:3–4+, October 1967.

Cox, Pat, "Tony Williams: An Interview Scenario." *Down Beat*, May 28, 1970, p. 14.

Crawford, M., "Miles and Gil—portrait of a friendship." *Down Beat*, 28:18–9, February 16, 1961.

Crawford, Marc, "Miles Davis: Evil Genius of Jazz." *Ebony*, 16:69–72, January, 1961.

Dahlgren, C., "Gilmtar om glimtar." *Orkester Journalen Stockholm,* 22:22–3, December 1954.

"Dave Holland forms Circle." *Jazz and Pop,* 10:25–6, February 1971.

Davis, Miles, "Miles Davis." *Esquire,* March 1962, p. 59.

———— "My Best on Wax." *Down Beat,* 18:7, March 23, 1951.

———— "Self-portrait: Miles Davis." *Down Beat,* 25:17+, March 6, 1958.

———— "Self-portrait of the Artist." Biography from Columbia Records Press and Public Information, 1968.

"Davis-Charles at the Bohemia." *Metronome,* 72:8, August 1956.

Dawbarn, B., "Great Jazz Solos." *Melody Maker,* 41:8, December 3, 1966.

———— "Miles Davis is a Genius." *Melody Maker,* 35:2–3, October 1, 1960.

"Days in the lives of our jazz superstars." *Down Beat,* 37:11, April 16, 1970.

DeMichael, Don, "And in This Corner, the Sidewalk Kid. . . ." *Down Beat,* 36:25, December 11, 1969, p. 12+.

———— "Miles Davis." *Rolling Stone,* no. 48, December 13, 1969, p. 23–6.

"Disques du mois: Miles Davis at Fillmore." *Jazz Magazine,* n188:38–9, April 1971.

"Disques du mois: Bitches Brew." *Jazz Magazine,* n180:40, July–August, 1970.

"Disques du mois: Miles at Newport." *Jazz Magazine,* n177:44–5, April 1970.

Dove, I., Talent in Action. *Billboard,* 82:26, March 21, 1970.

"The Duke in Berlin." Port. (trans. and excerpted from Frankfurter Neue Press 11-11-69), *American Musical Digest,* 1:40 n4 1970.

Eckstine, B., "Dizzy, Bird, and the Birth of Bop." *Melody Maker,* 30:5, September 4, 1954.

Eniss J., "Miles Smiles," biog. port. *Melody Maker*, 46:16–17, January 9, 1971.

"Eric Joins Miles' New Rock Group." *Rolling Stone*, n61:10, June 25, 1970.

"The Evolution of Miles." Columbia Records, Press and Public Information.

Feather, L., "Blindfold Test." *Down Beat*, 31:31, June 18, 1964.

———— "Blindfold Test." *Down Beat*, 35:34, June 13, 1968.

Feather, Leonard, *The Book of Jazz from Then Till Now.* New York: Horizon, 1965.

———— "Caught in the Act." *Melody Maker*, 46:32, May 8, 1971.

———— *The Encyclopedia of Jazz.* New York: Horizon Press, 1960.

Feather, L., "Feather's Nest." *Down Beat*, 28:43–4, August 17, 1961.

———— "Jazz at the Crossroads." *Melody Maker*, 45:35, September 12, 1970 (port.).

———— "Jazz Records: Great, Greater, Greatest." *Show*, 2:102–3, February 1962.

———— "Los Angeles." *Jazz Magazine*, n189:11, May 1971.

———— "Miles and Miles of Trumpet Players." *Down Beat*, 22:33, September 21, 1955.

———— "Miles and the Fifties." *Down Beat*, 31:44–8+, July 2, 1964.

———— "Miles au 'Manne.'" *Jazz Magazine*, 154:15, May, 1968.

———— "Miles: A View From the Top." *Melody Maker*, 43:11, April 20, 1968.

———— "Miles Hits the Mood of Today." *Melody Maker*, 45:39, October 24, 1970 (port.).

———— "More Miles." *Down Beat*, 25:29, August 7, 1958.

———— "Moving with Miles." *Melody Maker*, 39:12, June 6, 1964.

———— "Now it's Miles the Mikado." *Melody Maker*, 39:6, August 8, 1964.

———— "Poll-topper Miles has been at a standstill since back in 1950." *Melody Maker,* 28:11, February 23, 1952.

———— "The name of the game." *Down Beat,* 37:11, October 15, 1970.

———— "The Real Miles Davis." *Melody Maker,* 35:2–3, September 17, 1960.

———— "That Birdland Beating." *Melody Maker,* 34:5, September 5, 1959.

———— "Tokyo Blues; Japan's Recent World Jazz Festival." *Down Beat,* 31:20–23, September 10, 1964.

———— "Voyages en Quarantaine." *Jazz Magazine,* 7:31, October 1961.

Ferrara, D., "The Trumpet." *Metronome,* 72:22+, July, 1956.

Finkelstein, Sidney, *Jazz: A People's Music.* New York: Citadel, 1948.

"Frisco's Masonic Temple Turns Down Miles Davis Benefit Show for NAACP." *Variety,* 222:1+, May 3, 1961.

"Frisco's Masonic Temple Drops Miles Davis' Ban; Feared 'wrong audience.'" *Variety,* 223:1+, June 14, 1961.

Frost, H., "Miles Davis." *Metronome,* 74:27–8+, May 1957.

Gardner, A. J., and Briestley, B., "Readers' letters: Miles Davis." *Jazz Monthly,* n183:31, May 1970.

Gardner, B. J., "The enigma of Miles Davis." *Down Beat,* 27:20–23, January 7, 1960.

Garriques, C. H., "Recapturing the Magic of Miles." *San Francisco Examiner,* October 11, 1959.

Gaspard, J. J., "Miles Davis." *Musica (chaix),* n67:29, October 1959.

Gerow, Maurice-Tanner, P.O.W., *A Study of Jazz.* Iowa: Wm. C. Brown, 1964.

Gibson, M., "Miles Davis—an appreciation." *Jazz Jl,* 12:7–8, June 1959.

Glassenburg, B., "Talent in Action." *Billboard,* 83:52, April 24, 1971.

―――― "Talent in Action." *Billboard,* 82:42, July 4; 21+ August 8, 1970.

Gleason, Ralph J., "Composed for 6 Months, Then Made Tune a Waltz." *Des Moines, Iowa, Register,* June 20, 1959.

―――― "Miles Davis." *Melody Maker,* 42:21, October 14, 1967.

―――― "Miles Davis." *Rolling Stone,* No. 48, December 13, 1969, p. 22.

―――― "Davis Quintet in its Totality." *Jazz and Pop,* 7:12, October 1968.

―――― "A Miles Davis Profile." *New York Journal-American,* August 20, 1960.

―――― "The Miles Davis Sextet All Play Miles-Way." *San Francisco Sunday Chronicle,* June 7, 1959, p. 23.

―――― "Mailer, Miles and Johnny Cash." *Jazz and Pop,* 7:12, August 1968.

―――― "Miles Was Waiting for Diz With a Trumpet and a Union Card." *San Francisco Chronicle,* January 26, 1958, p. 28.

Goddet, L., "La Chronique des Disques: Bitches Brew." *Jazz Hot,* n263:42, Summer 1970.

―――― "La chronique des disques: Jack Johnson." *Jazz Hot,* n274:29, July 1971.

Goldberg, Joe, *Jazz Masters of the Fifties.* New York. Macmillan Co. 1965.

Goldman, A., "Jazz meets Rock." *Atlantic Monthly,* 227:98, February 1971 (port.).

Goodrich, James, "On the Records." *Tan,* December 1954, p. 6.

Green, B., "Famous Last Words." *Jazz Journal,* 13:1 October 1960.

Grevatt, R., and Korall, B., "Probe into Birdland Beating-up." *Melody Maker,* 34:1+, September 5, 1959.

Grigson, L., "Directions in Modern Jazz." *Jazz Monthly,* 7:16–7, September 1961.

Gros-Claude, P., "Miles Davis à Wight." *Jazz Magazine,* n182:12–3, October 1970 (port.).

Grove, Gene, "The New World of Jazz." *New York Post,* November 16, 1960, p. 6.

Hadlock, Dick, "Caught in the Act." University of California Jazz Festival. *Down Beat,* 37:14, July 23, 1970, pp. 28, 30.

Harris, P., "Nothing but Bop? 'Stupid' says Miles." *Down Beat* 17:18–9, January 27, 1950.

Harrison, Max, "Gil Evans and Miles Davis." Pt. 2. *Jazz Monthly,* 5:10–12, February 1960.

———— "Miles Davis Concert Review." *Jazz Monthly* 6:14–5, December 1960.

Heckman, D., "Jazz: Optimism" (Excerpt from *Village Voice* 3-12-70). *American Musical Digest,* 1:16–7 n6 1970.

———— "Miles Davis times three; The Evolution of a Jazz Artist." *Down Beat,* 29:16–9, August 30, 1962.

Heineman, Alan, "Record Reviews—Filles de Kilimanjaro." *Down Beat,* May 29, 1969, p. 21.

Hentoff, Nat, and McCarthy, Albert J., eds., *Jazz.* New York: Rinehart & Company, Inc., 1959.

Hentoff, N., *The Jazz Makers,* Shapiro, N. ed., New York: Rinehart, 1957.

Hentoff, N., "An afternoon with Miles Davis." *Jazz Review,* 1:9–12, December 1958.

———— *Jazz Country.* New York: Harper & Row, Publishers, 1965.

Hentoff, Nat, "Miles." *Down Beat,* November 2, 1955, pp. 13–4.

———— "Miles (appraisal of today's jazz scene)." *Down Beat,* 22:13–4, November 2, 1955.

———— "Miles Davis." *International Musician,* 59:20–1, February 1961.

———— "Miles Davis: Best Rhythm Team Yet." *Hi-Fi/ Stereo Review,* 18:62, June 1967.

———— "The Singular Trumpet of Miles Davis." *Hi-Fi/ Stereo Review*, 15:86, December 1965.

Hess, J. B., and others, "Miles Davis: La Volonte de Puissance," ports. *Jazz Magazine*, n187:28–33+, March 1971.

Hodier, André, *Jazz: Its Evolution and Essence*. New York: Grove Press, 1956.

———— *Toward Jazz*. New York: Grove Pres, 1962.

Horfer, G. "Early Miles." *Down Beat*, 34:16–7, April 6, 1967.

———— "The Hot Box." *Down Beat*, 27:57, October 27, 1960.

Horricks, R., "A Milestone From Capitol." (LP) *Jazz Journal*, 7:34, December 1954.

Houston, B., "Great 'Jazz Solos." *Melody Maker*, 42:6, March 11, 1967.

———— "Miles Davis Talks About Birdland, Europe, Britain." *Melody Maker*, 39:16, February 1, 1964.

Idestram-Almquist, D., "Miles Davis." *Orkester Journalen*, 32:12–3, January 1964.

"Is Miles Quitting?" *Melody Maker*, 46:4, July 31, 1971.

Jalard, M. C., "Miles Aujourd'hui." *Jazz Magazine*, 9:37–9, October 1963.

———— "Notes Pour Miles." *Jazz Magazine*, 9:22–5, July, 1963.

James, Michael, *Miles Davis*. New York: A. S. Barnes, 1961.

———— *Miles Davis*. London: Cassell, 1961.

———— "Miles Davis," *Orkester Journalen*, 26:10–13, December 1958.

———— "Out of the Bag," *Jazz Monthly*, 8:16–7, 1962.

———— "Some Notes on 'Lift to the Scaffold.'" *Jazz Monthly*, 7:45, February 1962.

"Jazz Photos." *Down Beat*. 23:42–3, May 16, 1956.

Jazz trumpeter M Davis is arrested in Manhattan and charged with unlawful imprisonment and menacing of L Merker in his apartment on July 9, after allegedly preventing Mrs. Merker from leaving, *New York Times*, Jl 19, 43:2, 1972.

Jazz trumpeter M Davis reptd. in satisfactory condition on October 21 after breaking both his legs in auto accident in NYC, *New York Times,* O 22, 81:6, 1972.

Jepsen, Jorgen Grunnet, *A Discography of Miles Davis.* Copenhagen, N.V., Karl Emil Knudsen, 1969.

Jones, Le Roi, *Black Music.* New York: William Morrow & Company, Inc., 1967.

——— *Blues People.* New York: William Morrow & Company, Inc., 1963.

Jones, M., "Miles is Taking a Chance." *Melody Maker,* 35:8–9, October 8, 1960.

——— "U.S. Jazzmen Quiz Critics—'A bristling evening!' " *Melody Maker,* 36:10, March 18, 1961.

"Judge Finds Miles Not Guilty." *Melody Maker,* 34:1, October 24, 1959.

Kart, Larry, "Miles Davis—Caught in the Act." *Down Beat,* August 7, 1969, p. 28.

——— "Record Reviews—In A Silent Way." *Down Beat,* October 30, 1969, p. 20–21.

Keil, Charles, *Urban Blues.* Chicago: University of Chicago Press, 1966.

King, Carolny, "No One Trumpet Player to Be at Downer College." *Milwaukee Wisconsin Journal,* March 19, 1959.

Koechlin, P., "Miles Davis." *Musica (chaix),* n126:60–61, September 1964.

Kolodin, I., " 'Miles Ahead' or Miles' Head?" *Saturday Review,* 42:60–61, September 12, 1959.

Korall, Burt, "The Davis Phenomenon." *Saturday Review,* 51:50–51, February 10, 1968.

——— "Miles Davis's Band is a Laboratory." *Melody Maker,* 34:12, September 12, 1959.

Kosner, Edward, "Miles Davis Benefit—'My Present to Africa.' " *New York Post,* May 7, 1961.

Larrabee, Eric, "Jazz Notes." *Harper's,* 26:96, May 1958.

Lifton, Lloyd, "Miles Davis' Solo on 'Godchild,' " (transcription), *Down Beat,* July 10, 1969, p. 42.

Lindgren, C. E., "Mina Sex Stora Jazzminnen." *Orkester Journalen*, 19:26, December 1951.

"Live-evil recording reviewed." *Los Angeles Times*, January 2, 1972, sec. col., p. 32.

Lourie, F., "Record Reviews: Jack Johnson." *Jazz and Pop*, 10:45, July 1971.

Lubin, D., "Records: Jack Johnson." *Rolling Stone*, n86:44, July 8, 1971.

Lucraft, H., "Miles and the Band at the Bowl." *Melody Maker*, 45:14, July 25, 1970.

Lyttelton, H., "Miles Davis in England: Boor or Businessman?" *Metro*, 77:53, December 1960.

———— "Here's My Theory." *Melody Maker*, 35:3, October 1, 1960.

———— "Miles Has Rights, Too." *Melody Maker*, 35:10, September 17, 1960.

M. Davis—Article on furnishings in N.Y.C. home, *New York Times*, July 18, 1970, 16:1.

M. Davis concert revd. by J. S. Wilson; G. Bartz performance noted, *New York Times*, November 28, 1971, 82:4.

MacRae, Barry, "Davis/Shepp," *Jazz Journal*, 20:12, December 1967.

———— *The Jazz Cataclysm*. South Brunswick, New York: A. S. Barnes, 1967.

———— "Record Reviews: At Fillmore." *Jazz Journal*, 24:35–6, March 1971.

"Les malheurs de Miles: Le trompettiste a annoncé son intention de renoncer a toute activité professionelle." *Jazz Magazine* n191:8, August 1971.

Mallofre, A., "Scandale e Barcelone." *Jazz Magazine*, 150:17–8, January 1968.

Mathiev, B., "The Inner Ear." *Down Beat*, 27:47, May 26, 1960.

Mellers, Wilfred, *Music in a New Found Land*. London: Barrie and Rockliff, 1964, New York: Alfred A. Knopf, Inc. 1965.

"Merci, Miles!" *Jazz Magazine,* 6:22, December 1960.

"Miles au Pilon," *Jazz Magazine,* 7:15, July 1961.

"Miles Back in Action." *Down Beat,* 32:14, December 30, 1965.

"Miles Davis." *Newsweek,* March 16, 1959.

"Miles Davis Acquitted of Dope Charge." *Melody Maker,* 27:6, January 27, 1951.

"Miles Davis Acquitted of Charges He Assaulted N.Y.C. Ptl." *New York Times,* January 12, 1960, 8:4.

"Miles Davis 'Approved' For Bay Concert." *Down Beat,* 28:13–4, July 20, 1961.

"Miles Davis Arrested on Narcotics Charge." *Melody Maker,* 26:1, September 30, 1950.

Miles Davis: Concert with Septet, Fillmore East. Review. *New York Times,* June 19, 1970, 24:3.

"Miles Davis Freed on Bail." *New York Times,* August 27, 55:2; August 28, 10:4, 1959.

"Miles Davis Held, N.Y.C. For Assaulting Ptl." *New York Times,* August 26, 15:1, 1959.

"Miles Davis Is 'The End.'" *New Haven Register,* August 27, 1961.

"Miles Davis' Movie Music (recording)." Port. *Stereo Review,* 27:78, July 1971.

"Miles Davis Quintet." *Down Beat,* 24:31, August 8, 1957.

"Miles Davis Says 'Yes' to the Press." *Melody Maker,* 35:1+, September 10, 1960.

"Miles Davis—Shot by Unknown Assailant While Sitting in His Car." *New York Times,* October 10, 96:1, 1969.

"Miles Davis Takes New Bride of Many Talents." *Down Beat,* 35:10–11, November 14, 1968.

"Miles Davis to Retire?" *Down Beat,* 28:13, July 6, 1961.

"Miles Davis to Sue N.Y. City." *Melody Maker,* 34:1, September 19, 1959.

"Miles Davis Wows 'em at Vanguard." *Billboard,* 72:17, November 21, 1960.

"Miles Exonerated." *Down Beat,* 27:12, February 18, 1960.

"Miles Files." *Down Beat,* 27:13, March 31, 1960.

"Miles; Henderson joins the Sextet." *Melody Maker*, 42:6, March 25, 1967.

Miller, M., " 'Bitches Brew' und das Neue Afrika." Port. *Neue Musikzeitung*, 19:9, n4, 1970.

Miller, William Robert, *The World of Pop Music and Jazz*. Christian Encounter Ser., Concordia, 1965.

Millstein, Gilbert, "On Stage: Miles Davis." *Horizon*, 3:100–1, May 1961.

Mingus, C., "An Open Letter to Miles Davis." *Down Beat*, 22:12–3, November 30, 1955.

Morgan, Alvin, and Horricks, Raymond, *Modern Jazz*. London: Gollancz, 1956.

Morgan, A., "Music by Miles Davis and Lars Gullin; two long playing records. *Jazz Journal*, 6:21, November 1953.

———— "Retrospection." *Jazz Journal*, 5:10, June 1952.

Morgenstern, D., "Heard and Seen." *Metro*, 78:7, September 1961.

———— "Miles in motion." Cover port., port. *Down Beat*, 37:16–7, September 3, 1970.

———— "Sippin' at Miles', or a press conference in reverse." *Metro*, 78:8+, May 1961.

Mortara, A., "Coltrane (e altei); la crisi del parkerismo." *Musical Jazz*, 17:18–22, March 1961.

Napoleon, A., "Record Reviews: The Essential Miles Davis." *Jazz Journal*, 24:29–30, May 1971.

Nelson, Don, "Miles Davis Scores at Benefit." *New York Daily News*, May 20, 1961, p. 23.

"The New Miles Davis Sextet." *Down Beat*, 30:17, April 25, 1963.

Norris, John, "Heard & Seen: Miles Davis, Massey Hall, Toronto." Port. *CODA*, 9:42, November 11, 1971.

O'Brien, N. C., "Miles Davis." *Jazz Journal*, 9:9, August 1956.

Ohman, A. R., "Miles Davis Elegant Stilbildan." *Orkester Journalen*, 18:12–3, October 1950.

"One Pays . . . Another Gets It." *Down Beat,* 30:11, November 7, 1963.

Ostransky, Leroy, *The Anatomy of Jazz.* Seattle: University of Washington Press, 1960.

Palmer, B., "Records: Miles Davis at Fillmore." *Rolling Stone,* n73:54, December 24, 1970.

"Le Palais Merveilleux." *Jazz Magazine,* n104:30–33, March 1964.

Pellock, Carl J., "Police Probe Brutality; Cancel Jazzman's Permit." *New York Times,* August 27, 1959, p. 9.

Peterson, O., "West Coast Highlights." *Jazz Journal,* 24:12–5, January 1971.

"Plugged Nickel, Chi." *Variety,* 241:70, January 12, 1966.

"Polls and awards (pop and jazz)." Cover port. *BMI* (Broadcast Music, Inc.), p. 11–3, March, 1971.

"Post-Bopper." *Time Magazine,* 71:63, January 20, 1958.

Postgate, J., "The St. Louis Sound," *Jazz Monthly,* 14:2–6, April 1968.

"Pourquoi si méchant, Miles?" *Jazz Magazine,* 6:24–7, October 1960.

"Pourquoi si gentil, Miles?" *Jazz Magazine,* 6:17–8, November 1960.

Priestley, B., Record Review; Bitches Brew. *Jazz Monthly,* n187:16, September 1970.

"Quattro chiacchiere con Oscar Valdambrini su cinque trombettisti." *Musical Jazz,* 16:28, Aug.–Sept. 1960.

Race, S., "Birth of an Era." *Melody Maker,* 33:7, October 18, 1958.

Ramsey, D., "Record Reviews: Jack Johnson." *Down Beat,* 38:29–30, September 16, 1971.

"Recording Artists' Roster." *Down Beat,* 21:94, June 30, 1954.

Reisner, Bob, "The Titans XIII. Miles Davis." *Village Voice,* June 25, 1958.

Renaud, H., "Propes sur le premier concert Miles Davis a l'Olympia." *Jazz Hot,* 26:22–3, November 1960.

Rolontz, B., "Miles Davis Group is Strong as Ethel Ennis Debuts Well." *Billboard,* 70:5, July 28, 1958.

Russell, R., "Brass Instrumentation in Be-Bop," *Record Changer,* 8:9–10, January 1949.

———— "Miles Davis en direct au Shelly's." *Jazz Hot,* n262:7, June 1970.

Russo, B., and Lifton, L., "Jazz off the Record." *Down Beat,* 18:12, March 9, 1951.

Saal, H., "Miles of Music." *Newsweek,* 75:99–110, March 23, 1970.

Santucci, C., "Il Mestiere di Miles." *Musical Jazz,* 21:10–19, August–September 1965.

"Sauvage Agression Contre Miles Davis." *Jazz Magazine,* 5:13, October 1959.

Schuller, Gunther, *Early Jazz: Its Roots and Musical Development.* New York: Oxford University Press, 1968.

"Sextette New-Look." *Jazz Magazine,* 9:13, May 1963.

Shaw, R. B., "Miles Above." *Jazz Journal,* 13:15–6, November 1960.

"Shelly's Manne-Hole." *Variety,* 252:69, October 30, 1968.

"The Slugging of Miles." *Down Beat,* 26:11–2, October 1, 1959.

"Le Solitaire." *Jazz Magazine,* 7:24–5, August 1961.

"The Sound of Miles" (television film). *Down Beat,* 27:13, August 18, 1960.

Spellman, A. B., *Four Lives in the Be-Bop Business.* New York: Pantheon Books, 1966.

———— "Small Band Jazz." *New Republic,* v. 159, August 17, 1968, pp. 40–41.

Stearns, Marshall W., *The Story of Jazz.* New York: Oxford University Press, 1956.

Stenbeck, L., "Quo vadis, Miles?" *Orkester Journalen,* 28:8–9, January 1960.

Stewart-Baxter, S., "Miles Davis," *Jazz Journal,* 9:7, November 1956.

Stratton, B., "Miles ahead in Rock Country." Port. *Down Beat,* 37:19, May 14, 1970.

Szantor, J., "Record reviews: Bitches Brew," *Down Beat*, 37:20–21, June 11, 1970.

Tercinet, A., "Chronique des disques: At F:¯nore." *Jazz Hot*, n269:34, February 1971.

"This is what they did to Miles Davis." *Melody Maker*, 34:1, September 12, 1959.

Throne, F., "Microsoleo al Microscopio." *Jazz IERI*, 11:48–53, January–February 1960.

Trumpeter M Davis, who failed to appear at Newport Jazz Festival concert, says he never agreed to perform, telephone int.; scores festival producer G Wein, holding Wein used his name in hopes he would play so as not to disappoint his fans; Wein says Davis accepted date and deposit against fee, *New York Times*, Jl 5, 31:6, 1972.

Turley, P., "Miles (recording Miles)." *Jazz*, 2:11+, June, 1963.

Tynan, J., "Caught in the Act." *Down Beat*, 27:42, April 14, 1960.

Tynan, Kenneth, "Miles Apart." *Holiday*, 33:101–3, February 1963.

Ulanov, Barry, *A Handbook of Jazz*. New York: The Viking Press, 1957.

——— *A History of Jazz in America*. New York: The Viking Press, 1952.

——— "Miles and Leo." *Metronome*, LXIII, July 1947, p. 19.

"U.S.A.–intervju i fick format: Miles Davis." *Orkester Journalen*, 19:8, May 1951.

Vartan, E., "Miles Davis, le solitaire." *Jazz Magazine*, 6:20–25, March 1960.

"Village Gate, N.Y." *Variety*, 251:52, July 24, 1968.

"Village Vanguard, N.Y." *Variety*, 220:60, November 23, 1960.

"Village Vanguard, N.Y." *Variety*, 222:67, March 8, 1961.

"Village Vanguard, N.Y." *Variety*, 231:74, July 17, 1963.

Vitet, Bernard, "Miles Davis I. Un Styliste en Constant Evolution." *Jazz Hot*, 26:10–13, April 1960.

———— "II. Miles Davis: The Man I Love." *Jazz Hot*, 26:12–13, May 1960.

———— "Miles Davis (III)." *Jazz Hot*, 26:12–3, June 1960.

Wagner, J., "Voici Miles, L'iconoclaste (interview)." *Jazz Magazine*, 9:26–31, April 1963.

Watts, M., "Weekend of Jazz Giants." *Melody Maker*, 46:25, November 20, 1971.

"West Coast Highlights. O. Peterson." *Jazz Journal*, 24:12–5+, January 1971.

Williams, Martin T., ed., *The Art of Jazz*. New York: Oxford University Press, 1959.

———— "Extended Improvisations and Form: Some Solutions," *Jazz Review*, 1:13–5+, December 1958.

———— *The Jazz Tradition*. New York: Oxford University Press, 1970.

———— "Miles Davis." *Saturday Review*, October 25, 1969, p. 75.

———— "Miles Davis A Man Walking." *Saturday Review*, 45:54–5, August 20, 1962.

———— "Miles Davis: Conception in Search of a Sound." *Jazz*, 4:8–11, 1965.

———— "Mostly Modernists: Miles Davis." *Saturday Review*, v. 52, October 25, 1969, ill., p. 75.

———— "The Public Miles Davis." *Saturday Review*, 47:72–3, September 26, 1964.

———— "Rollins and Davis Renewed." *Saturday Review*, 48:91, October 30, 1965.

———— *Where's the Melody?* New York: Pantheon Books, 1966.

Williams, R., "Jack Johnson (recording)." Port. *Melody Maker*, 46:26, May 29, 1971.

———— "Jazz Records: Miles at Fillmore." Port. *Melody Maker*, 46:26, January 16, 1971.

———— "What Made Miles Davis Go Pop?" Port. *Melody Maker*, 45:20–21, June 13, 1970.

Williams, R., and others, "Five Days That Rocked Britain." Port. *Melody Maker*, 45:25–6, September 5, 1970.

Wilmer, V., "Caught in the Act: Berlin Jazz Days." *Down Beat*, 37:26, January 22, 1970.

Wilson, J. S., "Promising Jazz Talents Fulfilled." *New York Times*, 107:11 (Sect. 2), January 12, 1958.

Wilson, Russ, "Columbia Records Signs Miles Davis." *Oakland Tribune*, February 4, 1956.

Winner, L., "Records: Bitches Brew." Port. *Rolling Stone*, n59:50, May 28, 1970.

Wood, B., "Miles Davis," *Jazz Journal*, 9:25+, May 1956.

Zwerin, M., "Miles Davis, A Most Curious Friendship." *Down Beat* 33:18–9+, March 10, 1966.

TRANSCRIPTIONS

This collection of thirteen transcriptions represents a span of twenty years in Miles Davis' professional career. Two pieces are from the late forties, seven from the fifties, and four from the sixties ("Sanctuary" was recorded in 1969 but released in 1970). I was especially interested in including some of his work from the large orchestra sessions, at least one live performance, and his two classics, "Walkin'" and "Solar." Outside of these considerations, the selections corresponded to the development of his career. They were transcribed at the piano with the rhythms worked out separately and then connected to the melodic lines. They adhere to concert key but can be freely transposed by anyone wishing to do so. I purposely left out the progressions because I believe that the hallmark of Miles's work lies in the structure of his dialoguing rhythms. This is not to say that Miles is not a giant of a harmonic, melodic player, but his sense of duration got him over.

One transcription, "Solar," begins on the first note of his first improvised chorus. The others begin where Miles starts playing. These transcriptions are only one small aspect of his improvisations. Nothing which is literate can adequately articulate the nuances of a nonliterate art form. The nuances of Miles's work are the particulars which make him an outstanding musician. These nuances include the numerous subtle mechanisms which he consistently uses to penetrate his listener like phenol: the lay-backs, smears, grace notes, and, mostly, the intensity with which he approaches any piece. So just looking at these transcriptions without listening to the music is simply missing the point.

JERU *(Recorded January 21, 1949)*

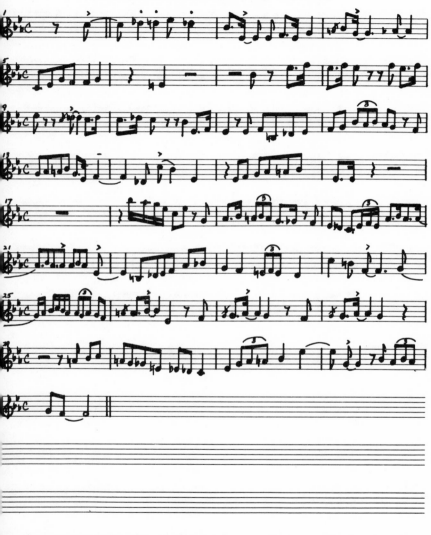

MOVE   *(Recorded January 21, 1949)*

DOWN   *(Recorded January 17, 1951)*

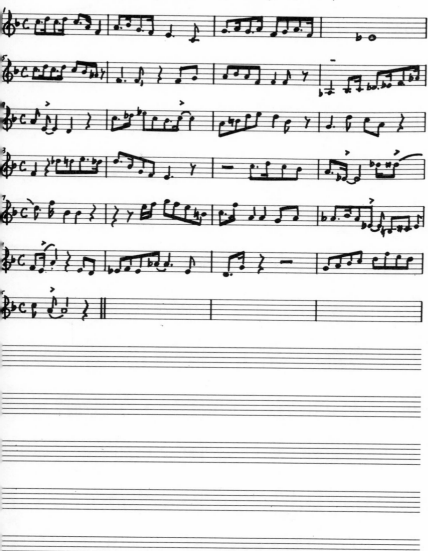

SOLAR   *(Recorded April 3, 1954)*

SOLAR (2)

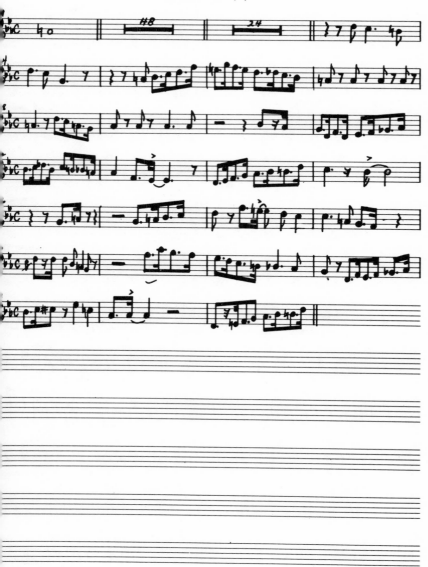

WALKIN' *(Recorded April 29, 1954)*

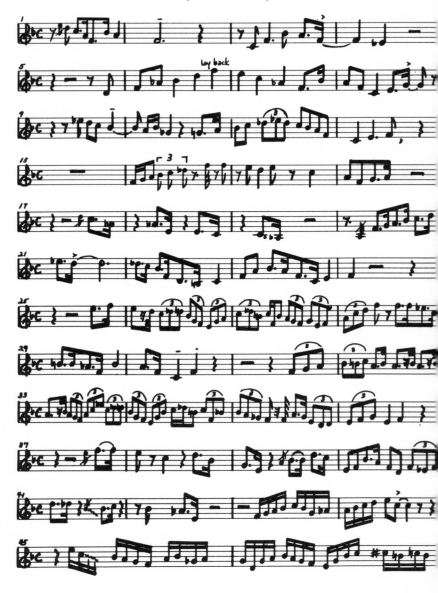

WALKIN' (2)

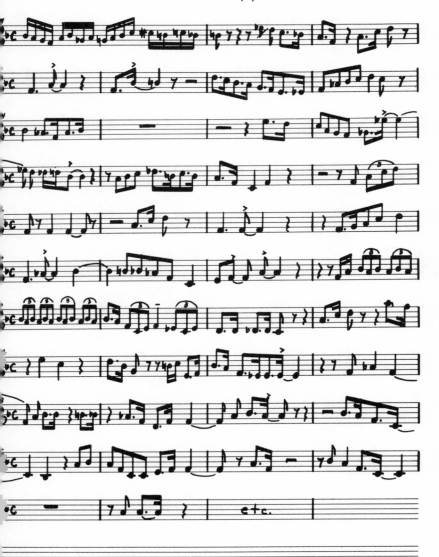

SPRINGSVILLE *(Recorded May 23, 1957)*

SPRINGSVILLE (2)

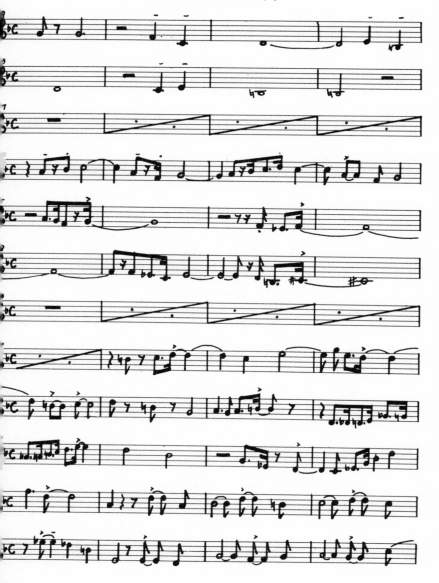

SPRINGSVILLE   (3)

SPRINGSVILLE (4)

SID'S AHEAD　*(Recorded April 3, 1958)*

SID'S AHEAD (2)

BLUE IN GREEN   *(Recorded March 2, 1959)*

SUMMERTIME *(Recorded August 18, 1958)*

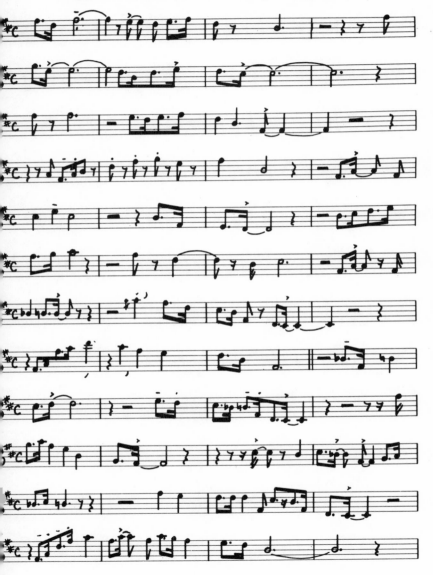

SUMMERTIME   (2)

MY FUNNY VALENTINE *(Recorded February 12, 1964)*

MY FUNNY VALENTINE (2)

MY FUNNY VALENTINE   *(3)*

CIRCLE *(Recorded October 24, 1966)*

CIRCLE (2)

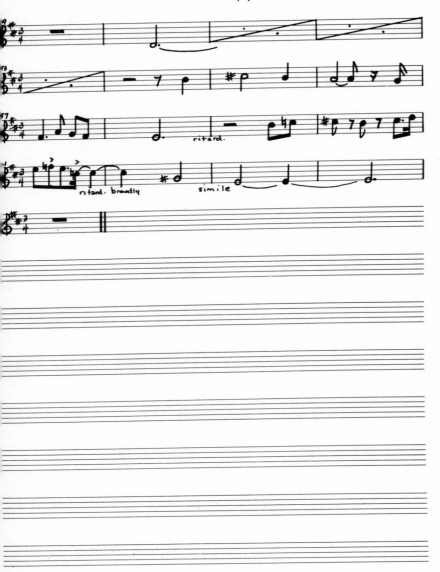

IN A SILENT WAY   (Recorded February 18, 1969)

SANCTUARY *(Recorded August 1969)*

SANCTUARY (2)

Index

247